SEPTEMBER 2

TO WHIT AYRES,

THANK YOU FOR YOUR
ENTHUSIASTIC PRESENTATION
TO THE GA. CHAMBER
EXECS IN D.C.

YOU ARE A GREAT
TEACHER, I MAY CALL
ON YOU FOR SOME
POLLING FOR ME ONE
DAY.

Donald E. Cole

Grassroots: Leading Others to Accomplish the Impossible

Sonny Perdue's Stunning Upset Victory as the First Republican to be Elected as Governor of Georgia in Over 130 Years

By
Donald E. Cole

Copyright © 2003 by Donald E. Cole

Printed in USA

International Standard Book Number – 0-9669289-8-9
Library of Congress Control Number: 2002117873

Front cover photo by Anne Bass
Anne's Photography – Dawson, GA.
Phone: 229-995-5414   e-mail: abass@surfsouth.com

The Perdue for a New Georgia Campaign Office gave permission to use portions of the statewide updates in the Dougherty/Lee updates as printed in this book. See Endnotes for specific references.

For Copies of
Grassroots: Leading Others to Accomplish the Impossible
Go to
www.grassrootsbook.com

This book is dedicated to

The Honorable
Sonny Perdue
Governor of Georgia

and

Georgia's First Lady
Mary Perdue

Citizen-Servants

Gary Smith, Chairman, Dougherty County Republican Party
Spreading the word on
Election Day!

"While Sonny Perdue is from the Heart of Georgia and is now considered the Heart of the Republican party, Don vividly writes about the blood that flows through that heart and keeps it pumping! That blood is made up of thousands of grassroots volunteers from all across the State who indeed put blood, sweat and tears into this phenomenal political victory!" **Gary Smith, Chairman Dougherty County Republican Party**

Leslie Cole, Liz Schillo, and Dreau Tucker getting the word out about Sonny and other Republicans on the eve of the election.

"This book shows that with faith in God, working together as a team, and having a vision we were able to change history in politics in the state of Georgia." **Pat Tippett - South Georgia Republican Activist**

"This pastor, computer guy, and political grass roots worker understands better than most what it took to cause the Georgia political earthquake this year. Anybody connected with the Perdue campaign needs to read this work." **Norma M. Rogers, First District Chair, Perdue for a New Georgia, Former State Committee Member and Former County Chair**

Contents

Acknowledgements

I am grateful to my wife, Leslie. She has shown the patience of Job over the past year of this campaign. When she gets that weekly (or is it daily) call from the Republican Party wanting money, she tells them that she has already donated her husband to the cause. Baby, you were right, Sonny will be Governor before I finish building those bookcases. My son, Doug, has been an encourager and supporter. He will one day become a wealthy movie director and provide for me in my old age. My parents, Robert and Earline Cole and my uncle, Jim Cole exchanged e-mails and ideas with me all through the campaign and writing of this book.

Gregg Jones has grown to be a close and trusted friend. He has an astounding network of relationships across the state and proved to be one of Sonny's key fund-raisers. His wife, Jami, also deserves a medal for her patience. Gregg's parents, Jack and Dotty Jones, are among the most gracious, positive, encouraging, people that I know.

Pat Tippett inspired and encouraged me to write this book. Pat and I met at the Round Robin Republican event on Memorial Day 2002 in Albany. She was a real cheerleader for my Dougherty/Lee updates.

Gary Smith, Chairman of the Dougherty County Republican Party, has been a prophetic leader in Dougherty County. At the first annual Lincoln Day Dinner, Gary presented "Grassroots Awards" to three people: Don Cole, Gregg Jones, and Tommy Ragsdale. Ten months later, all three had played key roles in the

Republican sweeps across Georgia. Gary rebuilt the Dougherty County Republican Party. He is a masterful leader.

Corinna Magelund and Jackson Murphy were tireless workers throughout the campaign. Their enthusiasm, determination, and never-say-die attitude kept us going. You both are an inspiration.

The Young Republicans have been a shot in the arm to the Republican campaigns in Southwest Georgia. Dreau Tucker resurrected the organization at Darton College and helped to expand participation beyond the student body. Dreau Tucker, Deena Cheek, Alison Stephens, Tanika Lakes, Scott Sapp, Liz Schillo, Luke Miller, Chrissy Davis, David Lincoln, Kellie Marchant, Alane Marks, Austen Holton, and the other Young Republicans did a great job this year.

Alton Harpe was a traditional African-American Die-Hard Democrat until she met Dylan Glenn. She is now on the Executive Committee of the Dougherty County Republican Party. Alton always had positive words for the regular campaign updates and encouraged me to keep writing.

Lauren Williams moved with her family from Cherokee County to Albany in late September and started helping with the campaign in October. She and her mother, Vicki, and sister, Bonnie, made calls, waved signs, stuffed envelopes, and were regular faithful fixtures in the campaign during the final weeks. Lauren reviewed and made helpful comments on drafts of this book.

Gregg Jones and I spent numerous hours on the phone with Leigh Ann Gillis, Nick Ayres, Paul Bennecke, Julie Smith, Derrick

Dickey, and Chris Young on Sonny's campaign staff. Paul Bennecke's statewide campaign updates were a main part of the Dougherty/Lee updates. Thank you Paul, for giving permission to include those updates in this book.

I met Norma Rogers in Savannah as part of the official greeting team for President George W. Bush on November 2. Norma is a gracious woman who makes friends quickly. I appreciate her enthusiastic review.

Three churches had an influence on my writing this book. The Baptist Worship Centre where I served for over four years is a church of members who truly walk by faith. Their example of selfless service, undying persistence, and total commitment, has been a life-changing inspiration. Lifegate Church is a congregation who believes that Christians have a responsibility to be an influence in society. Men like Ben Barrow are salt and light in our community. Monday through Saturday, they practice the faith that they proclaim on Sunday. Gordy-New Bethel Baptist Church is a country church near Sylvester. They asked me to serve as their interim pastor in August knowing that I was heavily involved in Sonny's campaign. They have been very gracious and our time of growing together in Christ has been a blessing. It is refreshing to focus on Christ with fellow believers. Individually, some of us may have different political persuasions, but we find common ground in the One who stands above all opinions and philosophies.

I work as a Principal Consultant and Project Manager with an outstanding team of professional information technology consultants on assignment at the Marine Corps Logistics Base in Albany. Bill Baker, Chrissy Blackman, Jim Boggs, Chad Friar, John Nestale, and Denise Walters deliver the highest level of quality service to our customer. Managing Director, Sumeet Shrivastava, and Service Delivery Manager, Jack Brown, are part of the home office management team in McLean, Virginia. I am proud to work with you.

There are numerous photographs throughout this book. Many are group pictures taken at public events by Anne Bass, a professional photographer who has won numerous awards. The Professional Photographers of America selected her works from worldwide competition for publication. I appreciate Anne's offering her talent and skills to capture history on film. If you need a photographer, give Anne a call. I have made a diligent effort to identify each person who is clearly recognizable: Jon Ayres, Marshall Bailey, Scott Beeley, Kenneth Berry, Ty Bettis, Jim Boggs, Robin Brown, Deena Cheek, Doug Cole, Earline Cole, James Cole, Leslie Cole, Robert Cole, Chrissy Davis, Lila Everson, Bill Farnsworth, Sheryl Gamble, T. Gamble, Challis Garey, Paige Garey, Rebecca Greer, Beth Hall, Hannah Elizabeth Hall, Hollis Hood, Cameron Jones, Dotty Jones, Gregg Jones, Jack Jones, Jami Jones, Varsha Kamat, Holly King, James King, James King, Gil Klemann, Liz Klemann, Bruce Lambert, Melanie Lawson, Vint Lawson, David Lincoln, John Lovejoy, Corinna Magelund, Kellie Marchman, Alane Marks, David Maschke, Luke Miller, Marvin Mixon, Austin Murphy, Jackson Murphy, Eric Newman, Robert Newsome III, Carin Reese, Ed Rynders, Scott Sapp, Abigail Smith, Caleb Smith, Gary Smith, Alison Stephens, Dixon Tharin, Dreau Tucker, Jim Wallace, Allen Williams, Bonnie Williams, Lauren Williams, Vicki Williams, Rosa Ward, Joe Woody.

Introduction

Goliath fell with a thud that sent shockwaves across the nation. Sonny Perdue made history. He put his little hometown of Bonaire, Georgia on the map. The Governor's race in Georgia was not even a blip on the radar screen in national circles – until late Tuesday night, November 5, 2002. Rush Limbaugh, Sean Hannity, Tim Russert, and other nationally recognized political commentators were talking about a man who just months before was considered an unknown State Senator having no chance of being elected Governor. Georgians woke up Wednesday morning with the first Republican Governor-Elect since Reconstruction. Sean Hannity summed it up in four words, "The Earthquake in Georgia."[1]

Sunday following the election, gentlemanly Pastor Rastus Salter, along with every member, of Sonny Perdue's church, Second Baptist Church in Warner Robins, was wearing a pin proclaiming "God Did It!" Sonny did the impossible. He didn't do it alone. He did it by humbly inspiring others to join in the journey. Thousands across Georgia believed enough to invest a big chunk of their lives in a vision and a dream. This is my story – no, it's our story – of that journey.

I grew up in Bonaire. My church family at Bonaire United Methodist Church helped instill character and strong core values in my life. I can still remember the old gymnasium across the road from the Methodist church. The gym burned to the ground and ironically, the fire station now stands in that same vicinity. The Bonaire Elementary School opened when I was in the second grade. Mr. David Perdue, Sonny's uncle, served as School Superintendent for twenty years. When people spoke of "Mr.

Perdue" it was with an awesome reverence, almost like being in church.

Sonny's mother, Miss Ophie, was a teacher. I don't know how many years she taught school, but it seems like she taught half the state of Georgia at one time or another. She taught me in high school and I have friends old enough to be my grandparents who had Miss Ophie as a teacher. Sonny was raised with a strong heritage of serving others.

Sonny was one of the older boys when I was growing up in Bonaire. He left for college when I was in elementary school. When he returned to Bonaire, I was in the Army. I really got to know Sonny after he went to the State Senate.

I started taking my son, Doug, to the State Capitol every year from the time he was 5 years old, to watch the legislature in session. I was serving as Pastor of Roberta Baptist Church in Roberta, Georgia. My calling led me into an overseas ministry in the Panama Canal community for several years so our annual trips to Atlanta were put on hold until 1995 when we moved back to the United States and settled in Albany, Georgia. On my first visit to the Senate after several years, I looked up our State Senator, Mark Taylor and asked Mark if he would re-introduce me to Sonny Perdue. Mark said that Sonny was the Senate Majority Leader and was one of the most respected members of the Senate. When I met Sonny and told him who I was, his first comment was about my mother. He paid her one of the highest compliments anyone could receive when he said, "Miss Earline is the conscience of Bonaire."

I grew to respect and admire Sonny Perdue more each time we met and talked. Sometimes we talked politics and sometimes we talked about family and ministry. Sonny's son served as Youth Pastor of Central Baptist Church in Athens and was planning to attend seminary. He had decisions to make and Sonny was interested in my perspective. Sonny was a counselor to me as well during some of those times.

When Sonny changed parties in 1998 he gave up a prestigious and powerful position as president pro-tem of the Senate. He knew that it was not likely that Republicans would take control of the Senate and that his decision would cost him political power. He stood with his conviction. Sonny's decision to stand firm in his convictions moved him up several rungs higher in the ladder of my respect. Sonny may have lost the formality of a position, but he never lost the power of his influence.

Rumors that Sonny Perdue was considering making a run for Governor started to circulate in late summer, early fall of 2001. I told some of my friends then, "If Sonny Perdue runs for Governor, I will help him get there." I was honored to serve as Dougherty County Co-Chairman in the Perdue for a New Georgia campaign.

During the past year I have observed and learned from a great leader who inspired thousands of grassroots workers. In today's sea of change and challenge, we need leaders who will confidently take the ball and lead others to accomplish the impossible.

Hope and Vision to Accomplish the Impossible

"He doesn't have a chance." "Why are you wasting your time?" "There is no way to overcome the war chest of Roy Barnes." "You folks are dreaming." I heard those kinds of remarks countless times over the past year – and these are some of the milder ones. Anyone involved in the Perdue for a New Georgia campaign heard the same comments. We could spend a day swapping stories. In some cases, well-meaning friends uttered those comments.

Governor Barnes had amassed a campaign war chest that was approaching ten million dollars. He had money and power. Plus, Barnes was reputed to be ruthless in exercising his power. Political pundits said that Barnes was unbeatable. Rumors were floating that Barnes might be considered as a Vice-Presidential or even Presidential candidate in 2004.

There are always plenty of people who do not want to face disappointment so they never take the risk. They play it safe and want their friends to play it safe too. They rationalize and come up with plenty of good excuses. Are you facing a challenge? First, determine within yourself that the challenge is possible – even if it appears to be impossible. There has got to be something deep down inside that calls for action.

Governor of Georgia was never a position to which Sonny aspired. He was comfortable in his business and serving as State Senator from Middle Georgia. In the summer of 2001 a spark ignited a fire within Sonny Perdue that led him to step out of the comfort of his circumstances. The legislature met in special session to deal with reapportionment. Roy Barnes and the Democratic Party of Georgia had elevated gerrymandering to a fine art. They made no pretense. The sole purpose of reapportionment was to maximize Democratic votes – period. The principles of fair representation and continuity of communities fell on deaf ears. The resulting maps brought gasps of unbelief. While Republicans were crying foul, something else was going on deep in the heart of the quiet man from Bonaire. Sonny would later refer to the reapportionment as a criminal assault on the people of Georgia. Someone had to stand up. Like Gary Cooper in High Noon, that someone would be Sonny Perdue.

When David faced Goliath, he didn't think about how small he was or how large Goliath was. He faced Goliath with a confidence based on the invisible, but very real power of God. In the New Testament, the writer of Hebrews says, "Now faith is the assurance of things hoped for, the conviction of things not seen." (Hebrews 11:1) Sonny believed that the people of Georgia wanted what he had to offer. He believed that the people of Georgia could not be bought with slick television ads. He believed that he could defeat Roy Barnes. Most of all, he believed that his candidacy was a high calling, not merely a personal desire.

Sonny shared his hope and vision. He initiated a bold plan to organize a campaign committee in every county in Georgia. He could see in his mind's eye every county in Georgia with an active, vibrant, campaign committee that would impact the people in their home counties. He saw concentric circles of influence flowing out of each individual to friends and family across the state. Sonny knew that several groups were passionate about a cause to which they could be committed. He wanted each county to identify a point person in four specific areas of influence: Educators, Public Safety, Faith, and Local Business.

Some people look at the obstacles and do not see anything else. The Barnes machine was like a huge vacuum cleaner sucking up every loose campaign dollar available. Sonny saw something that very few others noticed. The huge campaign chest for Roy Barnes was not the Governor's greatest asset. In fact, it was his greatest liability. One of the first ideas out of the Perdue campaign was the simple phrase, "Power of the People versus the People of Power." While Roy Barnes was amassing dollars in a war chest, Sonny would be amassing votes through an ever expanding, interconnecting, network of relationships.

Close your eyes for a moment and think of a still, quiet, lake on an early morning. There has been no breeze through the night. The water is as smooth as glass. Clouds gather overhead. Molecules of water in the atmosphere accumulate until eventually the force of gravity overcomes a drop of water. The drop falls through the sky toward earth. A single drop strikes the stillness of the lake and shatters the glassy surface. A tiny wave moves outward in a symmetrical circle from the point of impact. More drops fall and the tiny waves are intermingling with each other and creating more waves. The image of drops hitting the water, creating tiny waves that hit other waves, creating more waves, is an image of the grassroots campaign that Sonny could see from the start.

Leading others to accomplish the impossible starts by focusing on the possible in the "impossible." The Barnes strategy leaned heavily on expensive mass media. Sonny's strategy focused on the personal touch and individual relationships. He could see making use of the latest technology to link people together across the state through Internet, e-mail, videos, and conference calls. He could see the perfect marriage of high tech and high touch to overcome the massive obstacle of campaign finances.

Sonny saw victory in his mind's eye. When David placed a stone in his sling and started walking toward Goliath, he saw in his mind's eye the stone flying through the air, striking Goliath between the eyes, and Goliath crashing to the ground. While the Philistines mocked and the Israelites feared, David had hope and a vision to accomplish the impossible.

Boldness with Humble Conviction

"He called the Governor a rat!" It was a combination of Saturday Night Live, Jay Leno, and David Letterman all wrapped in one video that lasted less than ten minutes. The video was not intended for mass media advertising, but rather as a tool for campaign volunteers to learn more about Sonny Perdue, Roy Barnes, and the issues at hand. A portion of the video was clearly a spoof that used satire and humor to highlight the shortcomings of the Barnes administration. However, there was another purpose behind the spoof – and it worked.

The initial reaction was a media firestorm. Fellow Republican candidates, Bill Byrne and Linda Schrenko expressed shock and indignation that the office of Governor would be so demeaned. Bill Byrne promised to send Governor Barnes a personal note of apology. While pundits were wringing their hands in righteous indignation, Sonny quietly explained that it was clearly a satire intended to make a point.

Make a point, it did. Within 24 hours, the web site, www.votesonny.com, surged in activity. One could almost count on one hand the number of complaints, while thousands wanted to see this video and find out more about Sonny Perdue. I wonder just how many minutes of television and radio time and how many columns of newspaper and magazine articles were devoted to hashing and re-hashing the "rat" video. Sonny paid not one dime for any of that time and space and suddenly, he was a force with which to be reckoned in the race for the Republican nomination.

"Perdue Camp Puts Barnes Ads on Own Website" the headline of the press release glared. The sub-title cleverly noted: **"Perdue Worried That He Must List Barnes' Ad $$$ as 'In Kind Contribution'"** [2] Governor Barnes spent millions on television advertising. Roy Barnes commercials started airing in late spring, months before qualification and the primary. Advertisements are designed to sell and increase the market share of a product or idea. At least that is the theory. The Barnes campaign had one little problem – the people were not buying. After months and millions spent on a multiplicity of television spots, Roy Barnes was in the same place, possibly even lower, in the tracking polls than he was when he started.

Remember the story of the infamous "Wrong Way Roy Riegels" of the California Golden Bears? He picked up a fumble and ran toward his own goal in the 1929 Rose Bowl contest between the Bears and the Georgia Tech Yellow Jackets. When the Yellow Jackets saw what was happening, they did not try to stop Riegels. Sonny took Wrong Way Roy even one step further by actually helping Roy Barnes spread his advertisements. The Barnes campaign called the move childish, but once again, Sonny attracted national attention and gained more free media.

Throughout the campaign, Sonny Perdue expressed confidence while at the same time he remained quietly humble. Boldness is sometimes associated with arrogant bragging similar to that which one hears on professional wrestling interviews. Humility is sometimes associated with weakness. Both views are extreme and erroneous.

The Declaration of Independence closes with these words, "And for the support of this Declaration, with a firm reliance on the protection of divine Providence, we mutually pledge to each other our Lives, our Fortunes and our sacred Honor." The signers of the Declaration took a bold step, which put their very lives at great risk. They soberly took the step without loud boasting but with quiet, humble, firm resolve.

Personal Touch

Sonny Perdue has a gift of connecting with people. He made several personal visits to Albany during his campaign. The crowds grew with each visit. Repeatedly I heard comments like, "He really knows how to work the crowd." The reason Sonny is so effective is that he is not "working the crowd." He is genuinely interested in each person he meets.

Something happens when two people look at each other and shake hands. There is a bond that impacts the mind, body, and soul. There is an acknowledgement of person, value, and worth. In a one-on-one or small group setting, Sonny connects. His ability to listen, to understand, and to communicate played a key role in his election as Senate Majority Leader, later as Senate president pro-tem, and now as Governor.

On one of his trips to Albany, Sonny made a stop by Palmyra Nursing Home to see a dear friend of mine, Mrs. Lila Faye Everson. Her grandnephew, Mike Everson, was one of Sonny's former pastors. After a short visit, Sonny prayed for Mrs. Everson and went on to other stops on his busy schedule. Mrs. Everson had no money to offer, no powerful position of influence, no favors to call in. She had neither carrot nor stick. Sonny's visit with Mrs. Everson wasn't just a campaign stop. In fact, no visit for Sonny was just a campaign stop. He spoke often of the blessings and joy of meeting so many people across the state. Sonny won the hearts of the people he met. His personal touch inspired enthusiastic, passionate, support.

Sharing the Glory - People Need to Be Needed

When you are part of a group picture, whose face do you find first? Go ahead, you can admit it. I do the same thing. So does everyone else. We need to have a feeling of significance and worth. We need to be needed. When you feel needed and important, you will support and help the one who gives you that feeling of importance. I once heard a story of a famous person who had a picture in his office of a turtle on a fence post. When asked about the meaning of the picture, he said that the picture is a constant reminder to him that he didn't get where he is today without the help of others putting him there.

Sonny Perdue launched a bold plan to involve thousands of individuals across the state of Georgia. By May of 2002, his campaign organization had recruited at least one chairperson for every county in Georgia.

Listen to Sonny Perdue address an audience. Without fail he will point out several people in the crowd who are part of the group. He will have some compliment or word of appreciation. My friend, Joe Martin, is an active Dougherty County Republican. We were in a meeting discussing various Republican campaigns and Joe made the observation that when Sonny Perdue goes anywhere, he surrounds himself with people from the local community. Sonny makes sure that local people are a visible leadership presence around him.

Jesus gave His followers a powerful truth when He said, "Give and it will be given to you; good measure, pressed down, shaken together, running over, they will pour into your lap. For by your standard of measure it will be measured to you in return." (Luke 6:38)

Our natural, human, tendency is to focus on and elevate ourselves. That self-centered tendency will ultimately lead to self-destruction. However, when you control that natural tendency and work to make others important, you discover that you do not need to elevate yourself. In fact, you grow to learn that your purpose in life is not to be elevated but to serve others.

Let me give you a word of warning at this point: Manipulation will not work. If you "share" the glory with others for the sole purpose of getting them to elevate you, the charade will not last. People are not stupid. Insincere words quickly fade and any passing feelings of importance will turn to feelings of deep resentment.

Sonny often commented on how humbled he felt by the outpouring of support. He constantly credited his supporters for the successes. His words are not shallow. They come from the heart of a servant-leader. Sonny led others to accomplish the impossible by letting them know how important they are and sharing the glory. It was not "my" victory. It was "our" victory.

Patience and Persistence

"We will win this war." After the atrocious attack on the World Trade Center on September 11, 2001, President George W. Bush addressed the American people. With a firm, stern, and uncompromising resolve, he promised that America would seek, find, and destroy the evil forces who were out to harm the American people.

Politics and war have some things in common. The term "campaign" is associated with each. Both attempt to enter a new territory, establish a foothold, and eventually secure and control the territory. The difference is that war is fought with bullets and bombs while politics is fought with ideas and philosophies. The goal of war is to establish control over a territory while the goal of politics is to influence a majority of people to establish a particular philosophy and approach to governing. Both war and politics demand tremendous patience and persistence.

Sonny Perdue was born in an era when, as the joke goes, "Democrat" was stamped on every birth certificate. The outcome of nearly every election in Georgia was determined in the summer primary. You could almost skip the November election because there was only one name on the ballot for all but a handful of positions. Republicans were generally associated with the Union Army occupation, the carpetbaggers, and the Great Depression. None of those three mental images brought warm and fuzzy feelings to the average Georgian.

I encountered an example of these powerful emotional associations when I called a dear friend of mine before the Republican primary. I asked her to vote in the Republican Primary for Sonny. She was very gracious but replied, "I am a Democrat. My Daddy told me that with the Republicans the rich get richer and the poor get poorer and not to ever vote for a Republican. I like Sonny but I never have voted for a Republican and I never will. I will do anything in the world for you, but don't ask me to vote for a Republican."

Just a side note: I thought the idea of "rich" associated with Republicans and "poor" associated with Democrats was ironic as Roy Barnes was outspending Sonny. Even though unopposed in the primary, Barnes spent more money on his campaign before the primary than Sonny spent during the entire election cycle.

For years, Republicans in Georgia had valiantly fought for and gained tiny islands of support, mostly in the Atlanta area. Georgians are a conservative and patriotic people and Republican Presidential candidates began displaying more of the philosophies that were in tune with Georgians. Somehow, voting for a Republican for President seemed more palatable – but on the local and state level, the idea of a Republican still did not agree with the average Georgian appetite. Republicans actually gained a plurality of votes in the 1966 race for Governor between Bo Callaway and Lester Maddox. A write-in campaign by Ellis Arnall left neither candidate with a majority and the Georgia Constitution called for the House of Representatives to elect the Governor if no one received a majority. The Representatives stood with the Democratic Party and elected Lester Maddox even though he received fewer votes. Republicans were disappointed, but they patiently persisted.

Sonny was elected in 1990 to the Georgia State Senate during the Reagan/Bush era. The Democratic Party on the national scene had moved far left; however, the Georgia Democratic Party managed to distance itself from the national party's liberal swing. Georgia Democrats successfully presented themselves as the conservative wing of the party. Republicans, under Ronald Reagan brought back feelings of optimism, patriotism, and strong defense. Georgians had elected a few Republican congressmen and even replaced the icon, Herman Talmadge, with Mack Mattingly.

A group of moderate Democrats led the national Democratic Party in a reformation to present themselves as more conservative and mainstream. Americans elected Bill Clinton as President in 1992 and the Georgia Democratic party breathed a sigh of relief. Republicans in Georgia made some gains, most notably Paul Coverdell's election to the U.S. Senate, but otherwise the Democratic Party of Georgia maintained a stronghold in state and local offices.

There was no political advantage for Sonny to change from the Democratic to the Republican Party in 1998. Republicans were the minority party in the State Senate and there was little chance that Sonny would remain in his position as president pro-tem if he were to become a Republican. In fact, when he did change parties, he lost all of his powerful positions and saw his office move from the Capitol building back across the street to the Legislative Office Building. Sonny may have lost his "position," but he did not lose his influence. While position may be of some importance, it is external. Sonny made a choice and paid the political price. He left what was then the winning team and joined the team with a horrific century-long losing record.

When I was growing up, we woke up each weekday to the Bill Powell Show on WMAZ radio. Bill had an oft-repeated slogan that became a part of the Middle Georgia landscape, "Keep on keeping on!" Bill is gone now, but I can close my eyes and still hear the sound of his voice. In five short syllables, Bill summed up the deeply held work ethic of the people in the heart of Georgia. The principle found in those four simple words formed the bedrock of persistence in Sonny's life. Sonny paid a political price, but he knew that he did the right thing. He gave up the temporary power of a position, and he strengthened the permanent power of his influence. He patiently and persistently kept on serving the people to the best of his ability.

Sonny was raised on a farm. Farming demands patience and persistence. I have the honor of serving as interim pastor to the people of Gordy New Bethel Baptist Church near Sylvester, Georgia. Most of our members are farmers. Rarely does a farmer experience a perfect season where everything happens exactly according to schedule. The weather is dry when they need the rain, and it rains when they need it to be dry. Cold weather comes too late or the warm weather comes too early. Farmers recognize that life is not perfect. They understand that they have just got to keep doing what they do and make the best of the circumstances they have. There is no such thing as a farmer who is not patient and persistent.

Accomplishing the impossible does not come easily. If it did, it wouldn't be called impossible. Republican candidates had lost the race for Governor every time they ran for the past 130 years. In 2002, the Democratic candidate was an incumbent with power, prestige, and more money than anyone could ever imagine in his campaign fund. Added to those mountainous obstacles were two other candidates for Governor in the Republican primary and a shift in the primary date from July to August 20. Almost everyone thought that the statewide primary would certainly lead to a run-off on September 10. The winner would be left with an exhausted campaign, depleted finances, and less than sixty days to overcome the overwhelming power and resources of the incumbent.

Three Republicans were vying for the nomination. Bill Byrne was the Chairman of the Cobb County Commission. Linda Schrenko was State School Superintendent and had been elected twice to statewide office. Sonny Perdue was a State Senator from the little town of Bonaire. Conventional wisdom said that there would be a run-off between Bill Byrne and Linda Schrenko.

Sonny initiated his campaign with a focus on Roy Barnes and the Governorship. He rarely spoke about the other Republican candidates for Governor. Some called it presumptive to run against Roy Barnes before being selected as the nominee. Sonny never allowed that criticism to shift his focus from the ultimate goal of the Governorship. He persisted in pointing out the stark contrasts of behavior and philosophies between himself and the incumbent. Sonny said that his goal was not to just be the Republican nominee; his goal was to be Governor.

A political campaign encounters constant change, frequent setbacks, and occasional moments when everything falls perfectly into place. How a candidate deals with change in a campaign is an indicator of how one will deal with the changes and complexities of governing. The old saying: "Patience is a virtue" is more than just a saying. Sonny displays a calmness and positive demeanor that penetrates a given situation and creates a positive atmosphere. His patience generates and renews the persistence to accomplish the impossible.

Standing for a Worthy Cause

Sonny came to the Georgia Senate to serve the people. He wanted to be in a position to do the best for his district and the people of Georgia as a whole. Senate leaders recognized his hard work, listening ear, and ability to pull people together. In a short time Sonny was Senate Majority leader. In 1997, fellow Senators elected Sonny to serve as president pro-tem of the State Senate, the highest office in the Senate next to the Lieutenant Governor.

Sonny observed something that did not fit with his character and deeply held beliefs. He saw that there was a significant focus on power and control and less of a focus on service. His spiritual values were also coming under attack as political consultants were advising him to shed his firm stand on right-to-life in order to gain votes. He felt increasingly uncomfortable with the Democratic Party and its unwavering support for Bill Clinton in the face of hard evidence of corruption and lying under oath.

Most politicians rationalize that they can be more effective in a certain position; therefore, do whatever it takes to gain and maintain the "position." Working with any group of people requires a certain degree of compromise. Sonny viewed compromise like a platform. As long as the platform was wide enough for him to stand with his deeply held convictions, he could make compromises on peripheral matters. He did not have to agree with every plank in the platform, as long as he could continue to stand firmly in the areas where he would not compromise. The planks were shrinking and Sonny could see that a day of reckoning was approaching. That day of reckoning arrived and Sonny took a courageous step of obedience to a high calling and deeply held convictions. On April 13, 1998 Sonny Perdue announced that he was changing to the Republican Party.

In the 1998 Senate, Sonny Perdue was president pro-tem and member of Appropriations, Ethics, Finance & Public Utilities, Health & Human Services, Reapportionment, Rules, and the Economic Development, Tourism, & Cultural Affairs Committees.[3] After the Senate adjourned and prior to the 1998 primary, Sonny announced that he was changing to the Republican Party. His constituency overwhelmingly re-elected him as a Republican. When he took his oath of office in 1999, Republicans were still the minority party. Sonny knew that he would not be re-elected president pro-tem. It was not surprising that newly elected Lieutenant Governor Mark Taylor would not appoint him to Chair a committee. The retribution for Sonny's "defection" went further than anyone expected. Sonny was not reassigned to any committee where he had previous experience and influence. His new committee assignments were Agriculture, Corrections, Correctional Institutions & Property, Defense, Science & Technology, and Special Judiciary.[4]

I have a sermon entitled "Rising to the Top." A key illustration and object lesson in the message is a jar containing beans and a couple of pecans. I turn the jar upside down so that the beans cover the pecans, and then I start to shake the jar. In the midst of the shaking and rattling, the pecans rise to the top of the beans. Turn it over, do it again, and the pecans rise to the top every time.[5] The principle is that everything in the jar receives the same knocks and shakes. The pecans rise to the top because they are larger on the inside than the beans. Character and integrity are internal strengths that do not depend on external circumstances.

I have shared that illustration with all ages. Even the youngest of children identify with the hard knocks. We all experience knocks, shakes, and rattles in life. In the midst of those knocks, each individual makes choices that builds character or dilutes character. The choice of patience and having the determination to persist builds strong character. Strong character results in growth.

Sonny Perdue established a campaign on sound and lofty principles with a focus on humble service. Sonny felt that the idea of service had been lost in the years of domination and power by one party. Representatives were pressured to follow a dictated plan rather than to bring the ideas and plans of their constituency to the table. In Sonny's mind, the Governor's race was not about Republicans or Democrats, black or white, rural or urban, rich or poor. It was about the worthy cause of public service. This was not just an election campaign – it was a cause – a cause worth the investment.

There is No Such Thing as a Bad Idea

Taking on an incumbent governor is a challenge. The massive war chest of Roy Barnes made the challenge even more daunting. A key word in Sonny's campaign was "innovation." The Perdue Campaign organized with an emphasis on bottom-up rather than top-down. The network of personal relationships was the key to victory.

A campaign organized from the bottom-up places tremendous responsibility and authority at the county level. Some might fear that overzealous volunteers would make statements or take actions that could reflect negatively on the campaign. On the contrary, the grassroots organization tapped a rich resource of ideas and innovation. As e-mail lists grew and communication across the state developed, people began to share ideas.

Fear kills innovation. Remember the times when you had a great idea to offer, but failed to share it? There was that mental image of everyone in the group (perhaps even everyone in the entire world), turning their heads and glaring as if to say, "That is the stupidest thing I have ever heard." How many solutions to problems have stopped at our mind's tollgate of fear?

There is a powerful chemistry that works in a group when people feel safe to share their ideas. The wise leader knows that every person holds a rich lode of ideas. Somewhere in all those ideas are valuable gems. A leader who creates an atmosphere that encourages brainstorming and freedom in sharing ideas will discover those valuable gems.

Grassroots: Leading Others to Accomplish the Impossible

Pat Tippett and Kay Godwin had an idea. What if Republican candidates for all statewide offices toured the state together before the primary? A joint effort would not only give each candidate more exposure before the primary, but it would also send a message that the Republican Party is a viable option. Pat and Kay scheduled what they called "Round Robin" events across Georgia. No one can fully assess the impact of the Round Robin events in the spring of 2002.

Corinna Magelund came to the Memorial Day weekend events in Albany and Thomasville. Corinna told me that she just graduated from Valdosta State University. She had an interest in working in the political arena. I told her that we couldn't pay her anything but we could give her some good experience. That same day she started as a full time volunteer on the Dougherty County Perdue for a New Georgia team. Three months later, Sonny hired her to coordinate volunteer efforts for the general election. Two determined South Georgia women had an idea. Their idea produced the valuable gem of volunteer involvement, which led to the recruitment of a valuable staff member for the Perdue Team.

T. Gamble is an attorney in Dawson, Georgia. One day Bill Whitaker stopped by T.'s office and made an interesting observation about some property on a major thoroughfare, Corridor Z, near Dawson. The Georgia Department of Transportation had inadvertently failed to secure title to a tiny piece of land, which happened to be located in the median on a small rise. The land was perhaps the most visible, strategic location on Corridor Z. T.'s first reaction was that the D.O.T. owned all the land within the right-of-way. After all, Corridor Z is a major multi-lane divided highway, extending from Columbus to Brunswick and thousands travel on it each day. T. researched the title and found that, in fact, Bill Whitaker owned the land. Within a matter of days travelers on Corridor Z in the vicinity of Dawson, Georgia were greeted with a huge "Sonny Perdue for Governor" sign sitting strategically on a small rise, literally in the middle of the road. If there were awards for strategic sign locations, that one should get an Oscar. One man's idea produced the valuable gem of high visibility and name recognition for the mere pittance of printing cost.

One of the most innovative ideas in the campaign came from a nine year old. The election was less than one week after Halloween. A common question to children around Halloween is, "What kind of costume will you have?" When Robert's mother asked him that question, he said, "I want to be a Sonny Perdue billboard." Hold your finger right here for a moment and turn to the newsletter article dated November 1, 2002 on page 172 to see a great picture. A nine year old had an idea that produced the valuable gem of innovative, attention-grabbing advertising.

Sonny Perdue has a gift of encouraging and motivating people. He does that by encouraging, appreciating, and recognizing the rich ideas and innovation of others. The gems of innovation, which lead to accomplishing the impossible, come from encouraging the exploration and mining of the rich lode of ideas.

Communication

Marriage counselors emphasize it. Management trainers emphasize it. Sales directors emphasize it. Communication. The ability to share ideas, directions, and information within a small group is a challenge in itself. Add to that, the challenge of communicating with an army of volunteer workers in 159 different counties across the state.

When Moses was leading the children of Israel across the wilderness toward the Promised Land, he had to learn about communication the hard way. His father-in-law, Jethro, paid a visit and he observed Moses holding court all day long. Moses was killing himself and not doing the people much good either. Jethro told Moses to organize the people into smaller groups so that Moses would only have to deal with the large issues. Moses organized the people into groups of thousands, hundreds, fifties, and tens. This new organizational structure vastly improved communication and made his life much easier. (See Exodus 18:13-27)

Sonny followed the game plan that Jethro wrote for Moses thousands of years ago. He established a professional campaign staff to help him organize the effort. Next, he identified and recruited chairpersons for each congressional district. Those chairpersons then identified and recruited chairpersons for each county within their district. Finally, the county chairpersons identified and recruited organizational teams within their own counties. Sonny's communication plan involved internal communications with his grassroots teams across the state and external communications to get his message and name out to voters in general.

My official involvement in the campaign started with a phone call from Gregg Jones. He asked, "Will you be the Dougherty County Co-Chair for Sonny Perdue?" Gregg and I had hundreds of phone conversations over the next ten months as we built a plan to get Sonny's message out to the voters in our part of the state.

There are many different means and levels of communication. The more personal and interactive the communication, the more the relationship is strengthened. The more the relationship is strengthened, the more commitment and involvement are enhanced. Internal communications with the campaign teams would consist of telephone contact, team meetings, and, internal e-mail updates. External communications would consist of weekly e-mail updates, yard signs, events, and telephone calls.

The telephone is perhaps the most efficient communication tool in use today. It seems that everyone complains about telemarketers but telemarketers stay in business for one reason only – they make sales or raise money. (When I'm in heaven, I will probably still be getting calls from the Republican National Committee letting me know that the President needs my financial support.)

We relied heavily on the telephone for team communications. E-mail messages are great tools for relaying information, but they do not communicate with a person at the commitment level. The growth of electronic communications over the past few years has led to information overload. Organizers of meetings and events will become very discouraged if they think that sending a fax or e-mail will be sufficient to get someone to attend.

Grassroots: Leading Others to Accomplish the Impossible

A few years ago, AT&T had a famous series of commercials with the message "reach out and touch." People communicate at a deeper level when they talk on the telephone than when reading a fax or e-mail message. Relationships develop and grow stronger when talking on the phone. It takes a little more time to make phone calls – but that is the point. We invested time in our team by making personal calls and the team continued to grow.

On a state level, the Perdue for a New Georgia team, used teleconferencing as a team-building and communication tool. Several times throughout the campaign, Sonny addressed the county committees across the state by means of a conference call. These calls unleashed tremendous power and enthusiasm. Committee chairs from Northwest Georgia were talking with committee chairs from Southeast Georgia. We encouraged and strengthened each other through shared victories and challenges.

The telephone is a great tool that combines two-way communication with convenience. Nothing; however, takes the place of face-to-face, personal, interaction. Our goal was to recruit and put together a team of volunteers. A team works together best when the members know each other. Many volunteers did not know each other prior to the campaign, but we all had one thing in common – we supported Sonny Perdue. We scheduled lunch meetings and called each potential team member personally. Team members made new friends and strengthened relationships. I noticed something taking place among those who met together. They encouraged each other and brought their friends to meetings and events.

The mutual encouragement proved to be a vital factor when we made telephone calls. The telephone bank was perhaps the most intimidating of all assignments. Telemarketers do not rank high on the list of favorite things for most people. Gregg Jones made his travel agency, Albany Travel, available for volunteers to call voters and encourage them to vote for Sonny Perdue. Most calls were well received and positive. In some cases the callers experienced hang-up or less than kind words. When a team member had a bad experience, we saw the value of working side by side. A few words of encouragement and a shared experience motivated the team member to make another call. The fact that we were together generated an atmosphere of accomplishment and victory.

Allow me to make a personal observation at this point. More took place than merely making phone calls. When one had a poor experience, another would encourage. When one had a positive experience, it spurred everyone else forward with confidence. Team members were challenging and overcoming fear. They experienced personal growth that would positively impact the rest of their lives.

Electronic mail seems like it has been around forever. It is fast, easy, and cost virtually nothing. When we started organizing the Dougherty County campaign committee, we made a conscious decision to send an e-mail update at least once each week. Even if the recipients deleted a message without reading it, the name "Sonny Perdue" would still be on the subject line. Paul Bennecke, Political Director of Perdue for a New Georgia, sent e-mail updates to District and County Chairs and other interested individuals on a regular basis throughout the campaign. We made a second conscious decision that we would not simply forward the updates from the state campaign. The Dougherty County updates would have something special to Dougherty County and Southwest

Georgia while at the same time, incorporating the information from the state office.

The regular and consistent updates proved to be one of the most successful forms of mass communication. We started including pictures of people actively involved in campaign activities in our area. The updates took on a personal touch and the list continued to grow. We were accomplishing several objectives through the regular updates. First, the updates helped to build name recognition for Sonny Perdue. Second, the updates portrayed a vibrant, committed, active organization. Third, the updates presented a confident assurance that "we are going to win!" Finally, the updates helped recruit others to participate.

Another major front in the communications campaign was yard signs. It was not hard to find people who were willing to have a Sonny Perdue sign in their yard. In fact, at one point, we had to stop promoting yard signs because we were running low. We did more than just make the signs available, we offered to deliver and place the yard signs. The effort required more volunteers and more time, but it produced tremendous results.

Jackson Murphy is a master of analysis and organization. He is a tireless worker. Yard signs are his specialty. Jackson has a keen sense about sign placement. He has the ability to make ten signs look like a hundred signs. The strategic sign placement at the beginning of the campaign established name recognition and presented Sonny Perdue as the leading candidate. Even in the general election there were more signs in Albany supporting Sonny Perdue than signs supporting hometown candidate Mark Taylor.

On the eve of the election, news anchor, Jon Williams and Darton College political science teacher, Roger Marietta, were discussing the campaign on the nightly WFXL news. The topic turned to the huge disparity in available campaign funds. Jon Williams observed that although Perdue did not have the money, one could drive through Albany and it seemed like every fourth house had a Perdue sign in the front yard. [6]

Conventional wisdom said that Linda Schrenko or Bill Byrne would be the Republican nominee. Conventional wisdom said that Roy Barnes had tons of money and no one had a chance against him. The Perdue campaign designed each phone call, each sign placement, and each e-mail update with the goal of chipping away at the conventional wisdom. Sonny determined at the beginning of his campaign that all communications would display the confidence of a front-runner. In Dougherty County, we wanted the voters to shift their thinking from "Sonny who?" to "those folks must know something that I don't." We knew that when people started to believe that someone could really beat Roy Barnes, then someone really could beat Roy Barnes.

People do not shift their thinking patterns overnight. In some cases the challenge was like getting a Chevy man to buy a Ford – not impossible, but close to it. We hammered away with weekly e-mail updates, strategic sign placement, and thousands of phone calls. The consistent and persistent communications chipped away at the conventional wisdom and helped replace it with a hope that Sonny Perdue could be the next Governor.

The Campaign Updates – They Tell the Story

Take a walk with me through history in the making. The campaign updates from the Dougherty/Lee campaign committees are a snapshot of what took place across Georgia. From the first letter to the editor on February 5, 2002 to the final update on November 11, 2002, you can watch Georgia history unfold before your eyes.

Sonny Perdue's election is a significant event in Georgia's political history. Republicans not only took the Governorship but also captured a majority in the State Senate. At the time of this writing, Republicans in the State House of Representatives are actively supporting State Representative Larry Walker as a bi-partisan candidate for Speaker of the House.

One day, Roy Barnes, Mark Taylor, and Tom Murphy, were running the show. The next day, Sonny Perdue is Governor-Elect, Tom Murphy is defeated, and the appointment powers and bill assignment powers of the Senate are being transferred from the Lt. Governor to the president pro-tem. Sean Hannity summed better than anyone else when he called it, "The Earthquake in Georgia." [7]

So, let's go see how it all happened.

The First Volley in Dougherty

People's Forum - Albany Herald – Tuesday, February 5, 2002

Sonny Perdue would be ideal governor

Georgians should elect Sonny Perdue as our next governor. Sonny is a servant leader. He is a man of integrity and strong character. Sonny has proven himself as a successful agricultural businessman and as a political leader.

He is highly respected by members of both political parties. He was elected by his fellow Senators to the office of President-Pro Tem of the Georgia State Senate.

Sonny understands the importance of agriculture and rural Georgia. He is a strong supporter of education and those who serve in education. Sonny Perdue makes decisions based on convictions, not political expediency. Most of all, Sonny is a citizen-servant.

He seeks the office of Governor, not for political power, but for the betterment of all Georgians. It is time for a fresh new day in Georgia. It is time for Sonny Perdue to be our next Governor.[8]

DONALD E. COLE
Albany

April 9, 2002

Dougherty County For Sonny Perdue

Sonny Perdue will be flying into Albany and holding a press conference on Thursday, April 11 at 2:00 pm at the Southwest Georgia Regional Airport. He will be addressing redistricting. Come to the airport to meet Sonny. This would be a good opportunity to bring a friend to meet Sonny in person.

If you have any questions, please feel free to drop me an e-mail.

Don Cole, Co-Chair
Dougherty County for Perdue

April 15, 2002

The Dougherty County Campaign Team for Sonny Perdue is gearing up to help move a new resident into the Governor's Mansion next January and that is none other than Sonny Perdue. We will be planning on sending out a weekly note on the campaign efforts in Dougherty County.

We are expecting victory for Sonny in November because we are confident that people across our state are ready for a change and are willing to invest in a victory.

If you haven't had the chance to meet Sonny yet, please read each one of these newsletters and look for an opportunity to go meet him. We will try to let you know when he is in Southwest Georgia. Also, keep a watch on the web site link below.

Sonny is a rare candidate for public office. He is running for Governor based on deeply held convictions of simple fairness, honesty, and public service. When you meet him, you will understand what I'm talking about.

Gregg Jones, 2nd Congressional District Co-Chair, is holding a fundraiser on May 14. The cost will be $125.00 per person. Keep in mind that Governor Barnes has a war chest of nearly 12 million. That may seem daunting and overwhelming, but I like the way that Sonny puts it when he says that he is confident that his contributors will vote for him.

Grassroots: Leading Others to Accomplish the Impossible

If you have any questions, suggestions, or would like to know how you can help, don't hesitate to reply and we will let you know how you can be a part of an historical election.

Thank you for your positive attitude and your prayers. Have a great week ahead.

April 18, 2002

Message forwarded from Sonny's Office
Progressive Ideas Like This Are Why Sonny Can Be Elected!

Perdue Announces Plan to Eliminate Income Tax on seniors

Will Grant Much-Needed Relief for Citizens Over 65, Make Georgia a Magnet for Retirees

HAZLEHURST, GA – Georgia Republican Gubernatorial candidate Sonny Perdue today announced his plan to eliminate state income taxes on Georgians over the age of 65. The plan would give much-needed tax relief to senior citizens and make Georgia an attractive relocation target for retirees.

Perdue told supporters in Hazlehurst, Baxley and Glennville today that he would submit legislation to eliminate non-wage income taxes on senior citizens on the first day of his administration. This was the first in a series of major policy announcements planned by the Perdue campaign over the coming weeks.

"Our senior citizens have worked hard, raised their families and paid their fair share of taxes," Perdue said. "Many of our retirees now have to live on fixed incomes and it is wrong to keep taxing them into their golden years."

Perdue also said that the tax cut would more than pay for itself by attracting senior citizens from other states to spend their retirement years in Georgia. These new Georgians would create jobs in housing and other industries and contribute to state coffers through sales and other existing state taxes.

A study by Dr. Richard J. Cebula, the Shirley and Philip Solomons Professor of Economics at Armstrong Atlantic State University in Savannah shows that the tax cut would generate revenue for the state within five years by attracting wealth to the state, encouraging consumer spending, and creating jobs.

"The cost of growing older is skyrocketing in America," Perdue said. "Eliminating these taxes on seniors is the right thing to do and I'm going to start that process before the sun sets on the first day of my administration."[9]

April 19, 2002

Forwarded from Perdue Campaign

Dougherty Team, you are a part of an historic campaign. This is the greatest organization of a grassroots campaign that our state has ever seen. Sonny's message is getting out and is getting people's attention. They like what they hear and will support. This campaign is about the power of the people prevailing over the people of power. If you know someone who would like to know more about Sonny, forward this e-mail and send me their e-mail address. Thank you for your support, your encouragement, and your prayers.

FOR IMMEDIATE RELEASE   CONTACT: Dan McLagan
Friday, April 19, 2002   770-220-0210

Perdue Campaign First to Organize in all 159 Georgia Counties

Only Statewide Campaign of Either Party to Establish Universal Grassroots Team; Steering Committee Tops 500, More than 2,500 Volunteers Register

ATLANTA, GA - The campaign of Georgia Republican Gubernatorial candidate Sonny Perdue today announced that it has established a grassroots organization in each of Georgia's 159 counties. This makes Sonny the only candidate of either party to have such an extensive team.

"It is unprecedented for a campaign to have reached this goal so early on," said Perdue Campaign manager Scott Rials. "There is a grassroots revolution brewing across the state working hard to send Roy Barnes packing and bring Sonny's new, open and responsive leadership to the Governor's office."

The campaign today released a list of its leadership team and predicted a victory of democracy and citizen involvement over big money and big government. It was also noted that Governor Barnes has apparently decided not to bother with courting grassroots support during the campaign.

"Roy Barnes has spent his time putting the squeeze on big-money donors, hoping he can buy the votes of Georgians with slick TV ads," Rials said. "He has ignored grassroots organization as he ignored the people of Georgia and their views for the past four years. He is about to learn a vital lesson about Democracy: it is people - not dollars - that count."

Rials also announced that Perdue's campaign now has more than 500 Steering Committee members and over 2,500 registered volunteers across the state. A leadership list of Perdue Grassroots County Chairmen and Steering Committee members follows.[10]

Perdue Campaign Team

1st District Chair: Norma Rogers
2nd District Chair: T. Gamble & Gregg Jones
3rd District Chair: Bill Bonner & Josh Bonner

4th District Chair: John White
5th District Chair: Edward Lindsey
6th District Chair: Bob Shaw
7th District Chair: Gene Sorrells
8th District Chair: Oney Hudson
9th District Chair: Denise Clopton & Dub Jones
10th District Chair: Jeff Davis
11th District Chair: Jim Ivey
Appling County: Pat Tippett
Athens/Clarke County: Michael Daniel
Atkinson County: Charles Lockwood
Bacon County: Leroy Carver
Baker County: Jimmy Rhodes
Baldwin County: Carol Grant
Banks County: Gerald Cline
Barrow County: Chris Bridges
Bartow County: Chuck Shiflett
Ben Hill County: Massee McKinley
Berrien County: Ed Perry
Bibb County: Trip Self
Bleckley County: Frank Scarborough
Brantley County: Kay Godwin
Brooks County: Mike Baugh
Bryan County: Michele Henderson
Bulloch County: Hal Roach
Burke County: George Deloach
Butts County: Patrick Carter
Calhoun County: Robert Toal
Camden County: Mike Zielinski
Candler County: Sean Sills
Carroll County: Mitchell Sayer
Catoosa County: Bill Clark

Charlton County: Kay Godwin
Chatham County: Carol Kaczorowski
Chattahoochee County: Joanne Ferguson
Chattooga County: Betty Brady
Cherokee County: John Wallace
Clay County: Buddy Durham
Clayton County: Vic Masserelli
Clinch County: Kay Godwin
Cobb County: Anthony Scott Hobbes
Coffee County: Sanilla Welborn
Colquitt County: Bill & Lynn Acuff
Columbia County: Nancy Bobbit & Rob Blandenburg
Cook County: Darvin Eason
Coweta County: Timothy Higgins
Crawford County: Sandra Neal
Crisp County: Jimmy Phillips
Dade County: Alan Bradford
Dawson County: Kevin Tanner
Decatur County: Dan Provence
DeKalb County: John White
Dodge County: Wayne Cartwright
Dooly County: Terrell Hudson
Dougherty County: Don Cole
Douglas County: Ken Bernard
Early County: Tom Beaty
Echols County: Phil Livermore
Effingham County: Larry Weddle
Elbert County: Ronnie Brown & Willene Grant
Emanuel County: Bobby Reeves
Evans County: Peggy Perkins
Fannin County: Scott Kiker
Fayette County: Chris Clark

Floyd County: Hugh Atkins
Forsyth County: Todd Tibbetts
Franklin County: Tommy & Mary Waldrop
Fulton County: Edward Lindsey
Gilmer County: Sam Burrell
Glascock County: Lee Griffin
Glynn County: Richard Wood
Gordon County: Carol Vogel
Grady County: Billy Hester
Greene County: Brian Burdette
Gwinnett County: Michael Murphy
Habersham County: Barbara Strain
Hall County: Al Gainey
Hancock County: Virginia Thompson
Haralson County: Norman Simmons
Harris County: James Woods
Hart County: Fred & Morene Sokol
Heard County: David Cagle
Henry County: William Woodall
Houston County: Larry O'Neal
Irwin County: David Martin
Jackson County: Mitch & Jean Mullis
Jasper County: Dan Jordan
Jeff Davis County: Ken Smith
Jefferson County: Leroy Lewis
Jenkins County: Dale Wiggins
Johnson County: Donald Smith
Jones County: Bill Cecil
Lamar County: John Martin
Lanier County: Ben Copeland
Laurens County: Jeremy Clay
Lee County: Scott Beeley

Grassroots: Leading Others to Accomplish the Impossible

Liberty County: Sampie Smith & John Ryon
Lincoln County: Derrick Dickey
Long County: Linda Deloach
Lowndes County: Bill Fuqua
Lumpkin County: Bill Grindle
Macon County: Roy Barker
Madison County: Hank Burnham
Marion County: Rex Icard
McDuffie County: Sara Lakey
McIntosh County: Ad Poppell
Meriwether County: Josh Bonner
Miller County: Russ Hanley
Mitchell County: Tim Pinson
Monroe County: Joan Thomas
Montgomery County: Luke Smith
Morgan County: Bethany Lee
Murray County: Rodney West
Muscogee County: William Rumer
Newton County: Art Williams
Oconee County: Nelson Holland
Oglethorpe County: Greg Jones
Paulding County: Glenn Richardson
Peach County: Sharon Berryhill
Pickens County: Bob Childree
Pierce County: Kay Godwin
Pike County: Ed Lynch
Polk County: Darroll Freeman
Pulaski County: Michael Sinyard
Putnam County: Martha Harris
Quitman County: Hugh Stovall
Rabun County: Dub Jones
Randolph County: Allene Nelson

Richmond County: Roy Reardon
Rockdale County: T. David Anderson
Schley County: David Theiss
Screven County: Osal Evans
Seminole County: Bill Fowler
Spalding County: David Knight
Stephens County: Kirby Rutherford
Stewart County: Rossie Ross
Sumter County: Mary Beth Bass
Talbot County: Bill Bonner
Taliaferro County: Jeff Davis
Tattnall County: Lamar Smith
Taylor County: Tas Smith
Telfair County: Ernest Dyal
Terrell County: Milton & Pam Foster
Thomas County: Scott & Lynn Sterling
Tift County: Rusty & Judy Simpson
Toombs County: Jim Collins & Mike King
Towns County: Tom Daniel
Treutlen County: Phillip Jennings
Troup County: Bart Smith
Turner County: Barry Barbee
Twiggs County: Charles Leavell
Union County: Vikki McVay
Upson County: Hoppie Hopkins
Walker County: Bob Clark
Walton County: Shirly Guhl
Ware County: Kay Godwin
Warren County: Dennis Coxwell
Washington County: Danny Brown
Wayne County: Sandra Harrington
Webster County: Grady Leverrett

Grassroots: Leading Others to Accomplish the Impossible

Wheeler County: Ronnie Williams
White County: Jerry Evans
Whitfield County: Phil Neff
Wilcox County: James Sutton
Wilkes County: Carmen Young
Wilkinson County: Gene Moore
Worth County: Janice Dent & Philip Greene

April 24, 2002

Many thanks to the Young Republicans of Darton College and other volunteers for their help in addressing invitations to an upcoming fundraiser.

Sonny participated in the Republican Gubernatorial Candidates debate last night in Cobb County. A similar forum is on the way to Dougherty County in May. We'll send updates for your calendar.

Want to help Sonny? Here are some ways you can help and be a part of this historical campaign:

- Canvassing Committee - canvass a neighborhood to tell people about Sonny Perdue
- Telephone Committee - call people to get out the vote on election day
- Sign Committee - Identify locations for signs and get permission from property owners. (Albany sign ordinances permit signs 60 days prior to an election and they must be on private property.)
- Addressing Envelopes - We prefer to have hand-addressed mail outs whenever possible.

Reply to this e-mail and let us know your area of interest. Forward this e-mail to your friends.

Grassroots: Leading Others to Accomplish the Impossible

We are continuing to build on communication and organization of the Dougherty County Committee. You will be receiving a weekly update of the campaign as well as any messages we receive from Sonny's state committee.

Thank you for your interest, encouragement, prayers, and support.

May 1, 2002

Personal Note from Don Cole, Dougherty County Co-Chairman

Last Monday, I attended a meeting in Atlanta with Sonny's campaign team and pollster. They gave some very good news and indicators from some of their early polling. Sonny sends his greetings to his supporters here in Southwest Georgia and is looking forward to being with us on May 14. See the key dates below. Sonny is more and more up every time I see him. People across the state are looking for someone who seeks office in order to serve instead of to be served. We all know that Sonny is that man.

Read the Declaration of Independence news release below and make note of the 4 actions Sonny is promising from his first day in office. Share these ideas with others. Keep up the great work.

Key Dates in Dougherty County

Tuesday May 14th, 7:00 pm: A fundraiser for Sonny Perdue will be held at Jack and Dotty Jones House. Please contact Gregg Jones for more information. 435-2285

Saturday May 25th, all statewide Republican candidates will visit Albany. Saxby Chambliss, Bob Irvin, **Sonny Perdue**, Bill Byrne, Linda Schrenko, and all other statewide candidates will speak at the rally. This will be a great opportunity to meet all the candidates and have fun and fellowship together! More details will follow soon! Please mark that date on your calendars and plan to come support **Sonny!**

Sign Your Declaration of Independence on the Web Link Below:

Perdue Kicks Off "Declaration of Independence" Tour of Georgia

"Government Belongs to the People, Not to One Man – We're Going to Take it Back."

LAWRENCEVILLE, GA – Georgia Republican gubernatorial candidate Sonny Perdue today kicked off a statewide "Declaration of Independence" tour in Lawrenceville. "We hereby declare our independence from four years of Monarchy and government by fiat from Roy Barnes," Perdue said. "We begin today a campaign to take power back from Governor Barnes and his royal court in Atlanta and return it to the people of Georgia where it belongs."

Perdue said that on the first day of his administration he would:

Have legislation introduced calling for new redistricting maps to be drawn which unite rather than divide communities and put people ahead of political expediency, appoint a statewide Inspector General to root out corruption at the state, county and local level and hold the first independent statewide audit in Georgia's history, introduce a bill to eliminate state taxes on non-wage income for all Georgians over the age of 65, begin closing the revolving door on legislators becoming lobbyists to schmooze their former colleagues, and friends, and Perdue urged citizens to sign an oversized Declaration of Independence document which he will take with him from town to town across Georgia – gathering names and support in his campaign to wrest power from a Governor many have called "King Roy." He also urged citizens from across Georgia to sign the document electronically through the campaign's website (www.votesonny.com). These signatures too will be added to the Declaration.

Today's event was held at the Gwinnett Historical Courthouse in a county named for Button Gwinnett – one of the signers of the original Declaration of Independence. Perdue also said he would be making a number of significant policy proposals as the Declaration of Independence tour travels across Georgia. "The Declaration of Independence tells us that the power of the government comes from the consent of the governed," Perdue said. "Government belongs to the people, not to one man – we're going to take it back."[11]

May 10, 2002

Sonny's Visit to Albany May 14

The next Governor of Georgia, Sonny Perdue, will be in Albany on Tuesday, May 14 for a fundraiser. Gregg Jones has been organizing a fund-raising event at the home of Jack and Dotty Jones. Gregg is experiencing an overwhelmingly positive response to the invitations.

Don't miss this opportunity to visit with Sonny and a host of Sonny supporters from Dougherty and Southwest Georgia. Call Gregg Jones at 435-2285. We are looking forward to seeing you there.

May 19, 2002
Major Event in Albany

Saturday May 25, 2002
3:00 PM - 5:00 PM
Veteran's Amphitheatre

GOP Candidates for Statewide and Local Races Will Be in Albany

Come out and Support Sonny and the Republican Party

Excellent Event to Invite Friends to Come Meet the Candidates

Be there to show your support for Sonny

May 23, 2002

Build a Better Mouse Trap and The World
Will Beat A Path to Your Door!

Dougherty County was well represented in Atlanta last Tuesday night to experience the world premiere of the movie, "A New Day Dawning" starring Sonny Perdue. Critics are raving about the movie and fully expect that there will be an Oscar in store for the best supporting actor - a very large rodent terrorizing classrooms, highways, and the gold dome itself.

Don Cole and Gregg Jones spoke with Nick Ayers in Sonny's campaign office today and learned that prior to yesterday Sonny's web site was receiving a few hundred hits each day. Since yesterday morning; however, they reported over 100,000 hits on the web site. Sonny has been contacted by CNN, Fox News, and numerous media outlets to talk about the video.

You can get the video directly off Sonny's web site at www.votesonny.com. It is a 10-minute video and you will need to download the QuickTime player. Please be patient as it takes a while. Gregg Jones and Don Cole have VCR copies of the video. If you want to get some friends together to see what all the talk is about, just reply to this e-mail and we can help you arrange a fun viewing.

Don't Forget About Saturday

3:00 - 5:00 pm

Veteran's Park Amphitheater

Republican Candidates for State Offices will be here

Sonny Will be Here as Well

Come out and Support Sonny

As well as our other Republican Candidates

See you there!

May 30, 2002

Republicans In Albany

Last Saturday we had a tremendous turnout to meet Republican Candidates for state offices. Sonny was there with a very positive message, which strengthened and added to his support in our area. Sonny is not from the Atlanta area and, being in agriculture, he possesses the understanding and compassion to remember Southwest Georgia. Several more new volunteers committed to work on Sonny's campaign in Dougherty County. Thanks to Gary Smith for his leadership in making this a successful event. WALB provided very good coverage for the event.

Video News

From Sonny's Campaign Office

More "New Day Dawning" Videos Available Next Week

We should finally be able to catch up with demand for copies of the much-talked-about "New Day Dawning" video when the campaign receives 7,000 more copies next week. We apologize for the delay, but requests overwhelmed our initial stockpile. We also apologize for the high traffic to our website which has made downloading the video a rather lengthy process.

Facts and Figures on the Video Release

Number of hits on website since release:	175,000
Number of copies downloaded (approximate):	1,400
Supportive emails:	650
Negative emails:	9

Examples of media coverage of the video:

- 10 GA TV stations (average of 3-4 stories each over several days)
- 15 Radio Interviews with Sonny (including Atlanta's "The Regular Guys" morning program)
- At least 20 newspaper articles (not counting editorials)
- CNN - Inside Politics
- Fox News (national)
- Fox News Bill O'Reilly (reportedly, we're seeking confirmation)
- The Washington Post

Strangest Request: came from the producers of 20th Century Fox's "The Simpson's" television program - Don't worry King Roy, it was for their personal enjoyment, not for use on the program... We think.

All Movies Have Reviews...

As a means to overcome Gov. Barnes' big money advantage - the governor had amassed $11 million at last count - the strategy borders on brilliant. After Tuesday's barrage of free publicity for the video, Perdue's campaign plans to post it on its Web site, prolonging its shelf life on office computers without spending a dime for TV advertising. [Macon Telegraph Editorial, 5/23/02][12]

Is all humor gone from politics? The rat's funny. And effective. When state school Superintendent Linda Schrenko, the governor's most bitter enemy, rushes to his defense, and his minions recoil in horror at the rat, it's clear that gubernatorial candidate Sonny Perdue's video is a twofer. Two zingers for the price of one. The clever thing about it is that Georgians are downloading it and passing it around. How do you compete against an incumbent who may have $20 million to spend? You just witnessed it. [Columnist Jim Wooten in the Atlanta Journal-Constitution, 5/24/02][13]

Perdue's campaign suddenly found itself swimming in attention: His Roswell campaign office was inundated with calls from CNN, the Fox Network and local TV stations. His Web site jumped from its daily average of a few hundred hits to 89,001 by 3 p.m. That's where the campaign mounted a downloadable 10-minute video that combines a Perdue biography with footage of a computer-enhanced, multistory rat stalking downtown Atlanta. The rat wears a crown, and a necklace identifying it as "King Roy." The narrator accuses Barnes of autocratic behavior, citing education reform and the state flag change. But the Perdue campaign insists it's all meant in fun. The video producer is Hollywood's Fred Davis who, for U.S. Rep. Bob Barr's 2000 campaign, produced TV commercials showing an actor portraying Democrat Roger Kahn bumbling his way through farm chores. [Atlanta Journal-Constitution, 5/23/02][14]

Linda Schrenko and Bill Byrne need to calm down. The Sonny Purdue rat video is absolutely hilarious. Schrenko and Byrne are just ticked off because they didn't have the imagination or the money to make the video themselves. [Neal Boortz's Nealz Nuze, 5/23/02][15]

"It'll shake them up down on West Paces Ferry," said Senate Minority Leader Tom Price, one of several legislators at the screening. [CapitolImpact.Com, CapitolImpact Georgia Report, 5/22/02] [16]

What's Next for Georgia's Newest Political Animal?

It's a big surprise, stay tuned.[17]

June 11, 2002

Into the Final Weeks Before the Primary
Dougherty County is Ready to Roll

On Saturday, June 15, the Dougherty County team will be going to Warner Robins with other 2nd District Chairpersons to meet Sonny and pick up campaign materials. The Dougherty County Steering Committee is planning several meetings to organize for putting out yard signs, walking tours, phone canvassing, and several other great ideas that have been presented.

Here are some simple ways you can help: (1) put a bumper sticker on your car. We want Sonny Perdue to be the most prominent name seen on the streets and in parking lots in Dougherty and surrounding areas. It is simple, takes no time, and gets the message out in a significant way. (2) Put up a Sonny Yard sign in your yard. When people see Sonny's name everywhere, they will tend to vote for him. Take a stand and let people know that you are behind Sonny all the way. (3) Ask your friends to let you put up a yard sign or to put a bumper sticker on their car. (4) Let us know that you are willing to be on a team to help canvas or call. (5) We need sign wavers for Election Day at several key precincts. Let us know that you can be on that team to help.

New Team Members for Dougherty

We welcome Corinna Magelund as a volunteer campaign staffer to our Dougherty County team. Corinna is a recent graduate of Valdosta State University where she was active in the Valdosta State University Republicans. Corinna is helping to plan and organize our team's activities. You can reach Corinna via e-mail at: cmmagelu@yahoo.com.

Beth Hall has taken the Faith Chairmanship. Her role will be working with local churches to let them know that Sonny is a man who lives out his faith year-round (not just at election time.) Helping her in that role will be Deena Cheek from Darton College. Deena will be the President of the Darton College Republicans next year.

Luke Miller has taken the Darton College Studen Chairmanship. His role will be promoting voter registration and promoting Sonny with the Darton College Student Body.

More on our team to follow in a future newsletter. We can use your help. Reply to this e-mail and let me know your area of interest.

Summary of Sonny's Platform - Share these ideas with your Friends

Education - Giving Parents, Teachers and Students a Voice

Governor Perdue will give a voice to parents, teachers, and students in public education. "Standards and accountability" are fine goals. But in the attempt to reach these goals, our current administration has implemented a "one size fits all" strategy and has added extra layers of bureaucracy to government. These extra burdens and regulations ignore the varying needs of our children around the state, stifle teacher creativity, and endanger the true education of our children. As Governor, Sonny Perdue will empower local schools, teachers, and parents to make decisions about their children's education. Our state government must accept the fact that parents, teachers, and communities know the needs of our children better than a disconnected bureaucracy in Atlanta.

Economy - Cutting Taxes & Paying Down Debt

Sonny Perdue has a strong record of fiscal responsibility in the State Senate. Perdue believes in "kitchen table" economics - state government should spend taxpayer money as responsibly as the people of this state spend their money. Waste should be aggressively cut and unnecessary bureaucracy should be eliminated.

Sonny Perdue supports a constitutional amendment that requires the use of surplus revenue for tax cuts or to pay down the debt. A 2/3 supermajority in both houses of the General Assembly would be required to use surpluses for any other purpose.

Small business growth is vital to the state's economic stability. Long-term economic growth in Georgia is dependent upon a business-friendly environment. Governor Perdue will be committed to reducing unnecessary burdens for small businesses-freeing them to create jobs throughout Georgia.

Tax Relief

Living on a fixed income plagues many of our seniors in Georgia - they have worked hard all of their lives, raised families, and are now enjoying their golden years. But health care costs are skyrocketing at a time when they should be reaping the benefits of a productive life of service. In order to give much needed relief, Governor Perdue will eliminate state income taxes on all non-wage incomes for Georgians over the age of 65. Perdue's plan will free up disposable income in times of rising health care and prescription drug costs.

Cleaning Up Corruption

Governor Perdue will initiate a statewide overhaul of state and local ethics laws. Georgia is growing weary of the corruption and scandals that jeopardize our citizens' trust in government. Governor Perdue will appoint a *State Inspector General*, charged with rooting out compromising fraud and abuses of power. The new Inspector General will be authorized to conduct Georgia's first-ever independent statewide audit. Finally, the Inspector General will lead the charge in a comprehensive overhaul of state ethics laws, including:

- The creation of a statewide Grand Jury-eliminating local conflicts of interest at the municipal and county level,
- A ban on lobbying by ex-legislators and former state officials for two years after they leave office, and
- A ban on lobbyists serving on statutorily created committees.

Sonny's ethics reform agenda will save taxpayer money from waste and corruption and restore the trust and faith of Georgia's citizens in their government.

A Visionary Plan for Traffic Relief and State Economic Development

Governor Perdue will lead the way as Georgia re-centers life around the home instead of the workplace. With universal high-speed internet access across Georgia, Governor Perdue will spread the economic benefits of a 21st century economy to all of Georgia, urban and rural. Using tax incentives and other public-private partnerships, Governor Perdue will:

- Ensure the development of a high-speed internet infrastructure to the "last mile" of service in every region of Georgia,
- Reduce traffic by making telecommuting standard practice in Georgia,
- Give families more time at home as life is re-centered on the home and not the workplace.

Georgia deserves a Governor with the vision to lead in the 21st century. Governor Perdue will set the stage for Georgia to compete economically-while relieving daily burdens on working families.

Redistricting-Returning the Power to the People

During his Inaugural Address, Governor Perdue will issue a forthright challenge to the new members of the General Assembly: draw a map that places the people of Georgia ahead of political parties and partisan politics. The district maps of our state should unite our communities rather than divide them. The challenge:

- Remove political data from the redistricting process - do not divide our citizens simply because they choose to vote Democrat or Republican in a given election;
- Reunite communities across this state - make the number one criteria in the process the preservation of communities and united counties.[18]

June 19, 2002

Sonny will be on a plane hop tour of Georgia over the next 3 days. He will be in the Southwest Georgia area Friday.

Come see a New Day Dawn Over Georgia...

Bring your family and friends to show your support for our next Governor. Each event will last approximately 30 minutes.

Statewide Qualifying Tour

Wednesday, June 19th

9:30- Atlanta- State Capitol Steps
12:30- Savannah- Johnson Square
3:00- Macon- City Hall

Thursday, June 20th

12:00- Gainesville- City of Gainesville Airport
3:30- Augusta- Hero's Overlook on Riverwalk
5:30- Athens- The Arch

Friday, June 21st

12:00- Cordele- WSST TV Station
2:00 PM Thomasville
4:00- Columbus- Airport

If you can attend any of the events, we suggest that you contact Sonny's office at (770) 220-0210 for the latest schedule update on the day of the event.

June 20, 2002

Report From Dougherty Trip to
Perdue Headquarters in Warner Robins

Last Saturday a team from Southwest Georgia went to Warner Robins as a part of an army of statewide volunteers preparing to flood Georgia with Sonny Perdue campaign material. Corinna Magelund, from the Dougherty County team, shared her reflections of the atmosphere and activity:

"The Material Pick-up Day in Warner Robins last Saturday was a great opportunity for county chair's and volunteers to meet each other, and show their support for Sonny. Sonny's team was well-organized and eager to load-up signs. Actually, two of his team members Meredith and Phil were so quick to help, and would barely let me lift a finger. Sonny came in the backdoor happy and singing "It's a _Sonny_ day outside…" even his charming wife Mrs. Mary came. He greeted everyone, and then spoke with the news reporter, and local papers. Later, what would have been a perfect Kodak moment, Sonny, Gregg, Lee, Bryce, and some others sat in a circle on the sidewalk discussing who knows what (hopefully our next move) as if they were on Sonny's back porch. That's one of the great things I love and admire about Sonny he is so down to earth and takes in everything you have to say. He doesn't say let's talk at my office; he wants to talk to you right then and there! He cares what the people have to say and he shows it!"

Corinna Magelund

The Dougherty County team has been busy talking with residents and securing permission for yard sign locations and will be organizing to put the majority of signs up in a single day. This campaign has a winning candidate, a winning strategy, and a winning army of supporters across the state. Southwest Georgia is a key front in this campaign. You are going to make the difference and be the edge to victory. The massive distribution of materials is an indication of the depth and commitment of our march to victory.

Here's what Political Director, Paul Bennecke said in a press release prior to the distribution: "The hard work of our grassroots team and the genuine excitement of volunteers all across Georgia is about to become a visual presence. As Sonny heads into qualifying, thousands of supporters are going to canvass this state and get our message out to voters."

On a statewide basis, here are some of the figures of what Sonny's campaign distributed last Saturday:

- 25,000 yard signs
- 100,000 push cards
- 15,000 bumper stickers
- 30,000 lapel stickers
- Copies of "A New Day Dawning" campaign video
- T-shirts
- Lapel Pins

"Television ads are nice, but nothing is more effective than an endorsement from a neighbor," added Bennecke. "All the TV spots money can buy can't override the word of a friend or relative."[19]

Grassroots: Leading Others to Accomplish the Impossible

Sonny's campaign established a grassroots organization in each of Georgia's 159 counties by April. The unprecedented organization effort has yet to be matched by any opponent - including Roy Barnes. I am proud to be a part and proud of each person helping in this great challenge.

June 23, 2002

Dougherty Meets Sonny at 2 Campaign Stops

Sonny Perdue was flying around the State of Georgia last Wednesday, Thursday, and Friday after he officially qualified for the Governor's campaign. Gregg Jones met him at his stop at the Cordele Airport on Friday. About an hour later, Sonny flew in to Thomasville for a quick TV appearance for Channel 6 news. Don, Leslie, and Doug Cole along with Lee Bass met Sonny in Thomasville. Sonny is very impressed with your commitment and wanted us to pass this on to each one who is helping.

The Team Grows!

The campaign team has held two meetings. At our second meeting we had two new volunteers show up. After the meeting, we met with another person who couldn't attend the meeting that day but wanted to be on the team. By Saturday evening we had two more new team members. Everyone is excited about Sonny and working hard spreading the word. If you are on the team, then reply to this e-mail and let us know how you would like to help.

The Signs are Going Up!

Albany and Dougherty County sign ordinances allow campaign signs 60 days prior to the election. Last Saturday morning, in between the much-needed rain showers, campaign team members placed signs in strategic locations in Northwest Albany. Corinna Magelund, Deena Cheek, Chrissy Davis, and Doug Cole worked together to place signs along Partridge, Nottingham, Westgate, and Old Dawson Road. In addition to locations where permission had previously been granted, the team knocked on doors and gained permission for several more strategic spots for sign placements. Jackson Murphy provided the following statistics from the Georgia Department of Transportation on daily traffic counts:

- Nottingham Way 17,376 (vehicles per day)
- Old Dawson Road 17,260
- Westgate 10,198

That adds up to 45,000 cars per day seeing Sonny signs in those 3 areas alone - and folks, we are just getting started!

You are doing great!

June 30, 2002

Your Vote is Vital

Personal Reflections by Don Cole

Someone said to me, "Sonny Perdue doesn't need Dougherty County to win the nomination, so people should vote in the Democratic Primary on the County Commission Chairman and State Senate races."

Let me put it crystal clear. Your vote is vital to Sonny. When you go vote on August 20, take nothing for granted. Go to the polls with the idea that you, personally, will decide if Sonny Perdue will be the Republican nominee for Governor. You can't vote for Sonny if you don't vote in the Republican Primary. If you don't vote in the Republican Primary, then you are allowing other Republicans to determine who will run against Roy Barnes. Your vote is vital. Take nothing for granted.

Never forget the 2000 elections for President. Thousands in the panhandle of Florida were in line or on their way to the polls in the central time zone when the liberal media projected Al Gore to win Florida – before the polls closed and the first vote was counted! As a result, thousands decided that their vote didn't matter and would make no difference in the election. They turned away and returned home without voting. Had those thousands cast their vote for George W. Bush as they had intended, our nation would have been spared the debacle of butterfly ballots and hanging chads. When they turned away from the voting lines without voting, they gave strength to Al Gore. They thought it didn't matter. It did matter. Every vote is vital. Your vote is vital.

Out on the campaign trail we hear very often, "anybody but Roy Barnes." The truth of the matter is that "anybody" will not defeat Roy Barnes. Sonny Perdue is the candidate to beat Roy Barnes. Sonny Perdue will get those votes that went for Paul Coverdell but went against Guy Milner. Sonny Perdue will get those solid Republican votes across the state and he will get the votes of those Democrats who feel betrayed by Barnes and are looking for someone to trust. Sonny is the only candidate who will generate the passion, the support, and the trust of Georgians to replace Roy Barnes as Governor.

Sonny needs every Republican vote in Dougherty County. Your vote is vital. Don't let anyone tell you that Sonny Perdue doesn't need Dougherty County. If you want to vote for Sonny Perdue in November, then vote for Sonny Perdue in August.

Don't let the rest of Georgia decide – Vote Republican, Vote for Sonny.

Sincerely,
Donald E. Cole
Dougherty County Co-Chair
Sonny Perdue for Governor

July 2, 2002

Dougherty/Lee County
Joint Special Projects

Sign Placement Continues

(Left to Right - Deena Cheek, Chrissy Davis, Corinna Magelund, Doug Cole)

Spreading Sonny over Dougherty and Lee County

Drive around Dougherty and Lee County and everywhere you look you see SONNY. Volunteers from Dougherty and Lee County have joined together and are doing a fantastic job! The visibility is rapidly building name recognition and it is making an impact. Sonny Perdue is THE candidate for Governor.

The team is covering so many streets that we can't keep track. Here are some figures from the major traffic arteries in the Dougherty County where we have signs.

Daily Traffic Counts

Byron Plantation Road (Near Church)	1,970
Westgate Dr. (Between Westover & Beattie)	4,786
Beattie Road (Between Westgate & Gillionville)	3,680
Old Dawson Rd (By Applebee's)	17,260
Old Dawson Rd. (By Doublegate CC)	8,000
Stuart Ave. (Midway)	9,771
Dawson Road (Between Lake Loretta & 3rd Avenue)	24,499
Whispering Pines (Midway)	7,457
Gillionville Rd. (In front of Darton College)	16,843
North Slappey Blvd. (By Food Max)	29,700
3rd Avenue (By Credit Bureau)	8,700

We don't have the information yet for Lee County, but we are getting there.

Join the Team On Our Next Project!

Want to be part of an historical election? Want to make a significant impact in the future of Georgia? Then, come join us as we call Republican voters in Dougherty and Lee County to elect Sonny Perdue in the Republican Primary on August 20 and again in November. This will be one of those once in a lifetime challenges and an opportunity to personally make an impact in the lives of Georgians.

Just reply to this e-mail and let us know that you want to help. We are organizing the calling lists right now. We will be meeting together in one place to make a simple call to Republican voters asking them to vote in the Republican Primary and to vote for Sonny. Come meet new friends, have a good time together, and be a part of something that you will tell your great grandchildren about.

The Patriotic Duty of Public Service

We are having a wonderful time together putting up signs and telling people about Sonny. In the midst of our good times, remember this one thing above all else as we work together in this campaign. You are serving your country. You are doing the work of a patriot. When you forward an e-mail or tell someone about Sonny, you are part of a magnificent process that has been blessed by God for over two centuries. When you register to vote and when you cast your vote, you are a patriot and sending a beam of freedom's light around the world. Kings have tried to topple this great experiment in self-government that we call the United States of America - but freedom still rings. We went through a great period of civil war - but freedom still rings. We have faced times of great prosperity and times of great economic depression - but freedom still rings. We are facing the challenge of our differences - and freedom still rings. We are under a cloud of potential terrorist attack at any time - but we do not cower in fear - and freedom still rings.

It is unfortunate that many view this wonderful freedom of self-government with cynicism and distrust. The freedom to govern ourselves is a precious freedom that is only protected when you exercise it. When you knock on that door and talk about Sonny - you are defending freedom. When you make that telephone call - you are defending freedom. When you forward an e-mail and ask someone to vote for Sonny - you are defending freedom.

Grassroots: Leading Others to Accomplish the Impossible

This election is about defending freedom in a very real way. I am proud to be in the army of patriots who are defending freedom. Keep up the good fight.

May God richly bless you and may God bless America. Have a happy Fourth of July!

Sincerely,
Don Cole

July 9, 2002
Dougherty/Lee County
Campaign Committee

Clockwise starting at front left: Marshall Bailey, Corinna Magelund, Deena Cheek, David Lincoln, Beth Hall, Gregg Jones, Chrissy Davis, Don Cole, Luke Miller, Dreau Tucker

Sonny's Statewide Team Connected, Coordinated, Committed

Last night several of us met at Albany Travel with Gregg Jones to join a statewide conference call with District and County Chairs across the state. The call started at 7:00. The system announced each new participant as they entered the conference. For almost 10 minutes straight we heard the system announce new participant, new participant, new participant. County and District chairs were reporting on the phenomenal progress of the campaign. Northwest Georgia talked directly with Southeast Georgia. Cobb County reported that at a recent Republican event in Marietta, the Sonny Support was everywhere. One county needed more signs; a nearby county would make an appointment to meet. It was inspiring to see such a huge effort so well connected, so well coordinated, and so well committed to elect Sonny Perdue as our next Governor.

As we participated in the call we saw more clearly how our efforts here in Dougherty and Lee fit into the big picture. A single yard sign is part of a message that is repeated thousands of times over across the state. Your phone call to a friend or forwarding an e-mail, is part of a grassroots communication network that is unsurpassed on a campaign of this magnitude.

Sonny Perdue is the candidate to lead Georgia because he is showing his innovation and ability to pull people together in the campaign. His campaign is a microcosm of his strategic vision of high-speed Internet connection for every citizen of Georgia. Sonny Perdue is pulling people together in his campaign with a vision. He is involving and encouraging common people to take part in the process of governing ourselves. He is sharing his vision and leading positively forward. That's just what a Governor ought to be doing.

Focus on the August 20

We are in the final lap of the primary campaign. The campaign committee continues to recruit and involve as many people as possible. If you want to help in any way, respond to this e-mail and someone from the Dougherty/Lee Campaign team will be in touch. Plan to vote in the Republican Primary on August 20. Encourage your friends to vote in the Republican Primary on August 20. There are other races on the Democratic ticket and voters can only select a Republican Ballot or Democratic Ballot. Remind your friends that the purpose of the primaries is for each party to select their candidates. If you run into someone who says he or she is a Republican, then encourage him or her, in a positive way, to help select the Republican candidate and let those who identify themselves as Democrats select the Democratic candidate.

Key Date

July 22 is the last day to register to vote in the August 20 Primary

Sonny in the Area

Saturday, July 13th- Watermelon Festival Parade, Cordele (9:00-11:00)

Tuesday, July 30th- Tifton Fund Raiser, (6:00-8:00)

Saturday, August 10th- Valdosta Fund Raiser (6:00-8:00)

July 16, 2002

"Georgia will lead the nation in quality of life for senior citizens by the end of my administration and become a magnet for retirees from across the nation," Sonny Perdue said. "Our mothers and fathers and grandmothers and grandfathers deserve respect, a break from the taxes they've paid all their lives and access to quality health- and long-term care in their retirement years." [20]

Dougherty Co-Chair Don Cole with Lila Faye Everson at Palmyra Nursing Home in Albany, Georgia. Mrs. Everson is the great aunt of Sonny's former pastor, Mike Everson and enjoyed a visit with Sonny several months ago. She prays for Sonny every day and tells everyone she meets to vote for Sonny.

Phone Teams Preparing

Dougherty and Lee are organizing for teams of phone callers touching Lee and Dougherty County. Join the team to encourage people to vote for Sonny. Reply to this e-mail and say you want to be a part. We'll schedule you in with a group of others. Be a part of this historical campaign.

Report from Cobb County

These last weeks before the primary, Sonny is focusing his efforts in the metro Atlanta area. Last Thursday, Sonny spoke at a statewide grassroots rally along with Republican National Committee Chairman Marc Racicot at the Marietta Conference Center. 400 active Cobb GOP members including every elected legislator from Cobb County gave Sonny a standing ovation. Sonny was honored to sit between lifetime Republican leaders, Alec Poitevant and Carolyn Meadows.

Sonny is making tremendous strides in the metro Atlanta area, but that does not mean that Southwest Georgia can relax. Every vote is vital on August 20th especially in our area. Rural Georgia will be the key to electing Sonny Perdue as our next Governor. Keep on doing the fantastic job that you are doing.

July 24, 2002

"When I want your opinion, I'll give it to you." 👑King Roy

"There is a grassroots revolution brewing across the state working hard to send Roy Barnes packing and bring Sonny's new, open and responsive leadership to the Governor's office." (Scott Rials, Sonny Perdue Campaign Manager)[21]

Make A Statement against arrogance under the dome!

Sonny's latest bumper stickers arrived in Albany and Lee County last week. It makes a simple and powerful statement, in a humorous way, which describes the attitude and approach to governing by the current administration. "When I want your opinion, I'll give it to you." Contrast that to Sonny Perdue's theme, "Government of the People, by the People, for the People." Reply to this e-mail to request your bumper sticker or call Gregg Jones at (229) 435-2285.

Sonny to visit Albany August 15

Sonny is scheduling a visit to Albany on August 15 in a final campaign tour around the state. If you haven't met Sonny in person, this would be a great opportunity for you. More details to follow.

Reflections on the Campaign to Date

It always helps to pause and take a look back to see progress and accomplishments along the way. Less than a year ago, Sonny Perdue made the decision to enter the race for Governor. He had little name recognition in Dougherty and Lee County. Roy Barnes, with a multi-million dollar war chest was considered "unbeatable." Other Republicans had announced their intentions to run for Governor. As we head into the final weeks of the Republican primary election, let's take a look at what Sonny has already accomplished in this campaign and why the Republicans should elect him on August 20th.

- Plan to eliminate income tax on non-wage income for Senior Citizens.
- Sonny campaign announced on April 19th that it had organized committees in every county in Georgia.
- Numerous visits to Albany and Southwest Georgia.
- Plan for Ethics overhaul in state government - appointment of Inspector General.
- Declaration of Independence Tour - "Government belongs to the people, not to one man – we're going to take it back." (Sonny Perdue)
- Produced the most talked about campaign video of the year - "A New Day Dawning" which was a humorous contrast between Roy Barnes and Sonny Perdue.
- Extensive Plan for Education to return the responsibility and authority to the local levels and free teachers to do what they do best - teach. The plan includes Sonny's commitment to work closely and positively with the new State School Superintendent - regardless of the new

Superintendent's party affiliation. (This attitude alone is enough reason to elect Sonny.)

- Plan to reduce taxes and paying down Georgia's debt.
- Visionary plan to reduce traffic in the Atlanta metro area.
- Visionary plan to make high speed Internet available to every person in Georgia, thereby opening economic opportunity for all of Georgia.
- Plan to call for the legislature to put Georgia's communities back together through a logical reapportionment process that is not based on party affiliations but based on communities of interest.
- Statewide qualifying tour.
- Massive statewide distribution of literature and sign placement.

Throughout this campaign, Sonny has met the people in numerous settings. On at least 13 occasions Sonny has met in forums with the other Republican Gubernatorial candidates. When people meet Sonny, they like him, they trust him, and they want him to be their next Governor.

Sonny's focus throughout this campaign has been on winning the Governor's race. With the help of thousands of people just like you, Sonny's name has become familiar and trusted. On August 20th, Republicans will determine who will carry the banner for the Republican's in the race for Governor. Sonny has been carrying that banner focused on the Governor's office for the entire campaign. He has led by humble, positive, encouraging example. That's why Republicans should elect Sonny to keep on doing what he has been doing so well - pulling people together, building trust, and working for a better Georgia. Keep up the great work!

July 27, 2002

The Phones are Ringing for Sonny!

The phone bank started to work last Tuesday and Thursday. The response to our calls on behalf of Sonny was extremely positive. The number of signs for Sonny has made an impact. It was a rare case to find someone who had not at least heard of Sonny. Many eagerly wanted more information and we had to order more signs to handle the requests of those who are saying, "I want a sign for my yard."

Thanks to Jon Ayres, Jim Boggs, Rebecca Greer, Gregg Jones, David Lincoln, Corinna Magelund, Alane Marks, Jackson Murphy, Dixon Tharin, and Dreau Tucker for being the first round of volunteers. Our goal is to call every potential Republican voter in Dougherty and Lee County to tell them about Sonny. Reply to this e-mail and let us know that you want to help Sonny. It is a great opportunity to be involved in an historic election.

Sonny to Visit Albany August 15

12:00 Noon - Southwest Georgia Regional Airport

Sonny will be making a campaign stop on August 15 at 12:00 noon at Southwest Georgia Regional Airport. Plan on coming to see Sonny. If you haven't met him in person or if you have friends that haven't met him, this would be a great opportunity. Sonny will be in the meeting room just off the main lobby. There is plenty of parking and the airport will validate your parking ticket so there is no charge.

Absentee Voting

If there is a possibility that you will be out of town on Primary Day - Tuesday, August 20, you can go to the courthouse and vote by absentee ballot. It is simple. You can also call your elections office for specific details on receiving your absentee ballot in the mail. For Dougherty County the number is 229-431-3247 and in Lee County the number is 229-759-6002. Be sure to request the REPUBLICAN ballot.

August 1, 2002

Sonny to Visit Albany August 15
12:00 Noon - Southwest Georgia Regional Airport

Sonny will be making a campaign stop on August 15 at 12:00 noon at Southwest Georgia Regional Airport. Plan on coming to see Sonny. If you haven't met him in person or if you have friends that haven't met him, this would be a great opportunity. Sonny will be in the meeting room just off the main lobby. There is plenty of parking and the airport will validate your parking ticket so there is no charge.

The Phones Keep Ringing for Sonny!

The phone bank continues to work steadily having called most Republicans in Dougherty and Lee Counties. The positive response continues to grow. The team has sent out over 100 packets of information to people who want to know more about Sonny and to tell others about Sonny. Sonny's grassroots organization, like a crop that has been planted and cultivated, is reaching maturity. The first fruits will be evident on August 20 and the big harvest will come in on November 5. If you want to be a part, simply reply to this e-mail.

Call for Volunteers from the Atlanta Office
We are in need of volunteers this Friday and Saturday!

We will begin our phone bank at our Atlanta Headquarters from 11:00 a.m.- 6:00 p.m. both days. We also have several projects that we need help with. The Warner Robins Headquarters is also running a phone bank this weekend at the same time.

On Saturday, we will have a float in the Old Soldier's Day Parade in Fulton County. If you would like to walk in the parade with us, please contact me at paul@votesonny.com or 770-220-0210. We will meet at the Atlanta headquarters at 9:00 a.m. and be back by 12:30 p.m.

Also on Saturday, we will have a sign canvassing team going to Gwinnett and Fulton. If you are interested in helping with that, please contact me.

We have an additional 300 volunteers working across Georgia this weekend by going door-to-door, running phone banks, attending events, and putting up signs.

Thank you for your support and work on behalf of Sonny.

20 days till the primary!

Vote August 20th!![22]

August 4, 2002

Beth Hall - Faith Committee Chair and Phone Bank Volunteer

Sonny to Visit Albany August 15

12:00 Noon - Southwest Georgia Regional Airport

Sonny will be making a campaign stop on August 15 at 12:00 noon at Southwest Georgia Regional Airport. Plan on coming to see Sonny. If you haven't met him in person or if you have friends that haven't met him, this would be a great opportunity. Sonny will be in the meeting room just off the main lobby. There is plenty of parking and the airport will validate your parking ticket so there is no charge.

First Wave of Calls Completed in Dougherty/Lee!

Dotty Jones - Phone Bank Volunteer

A small army of volunteers called over 4,000 Republican voters from Dougherty and Lee Counties to tell them about Sonny. The response to the calls was overwhelmingly positive. Follow up calls are scheduled for the week prior to the election. Thanks to all those who helped with planning and making the calls. Get ready for the second wave!

What you can do now

Primary Election day is about 2 weeks away. We have all worked very hard to get Sonny's name out and everyone is doing a fantastic job. Support for Sonny is growing rapidly. Financial support is also pouring in to help Sonny win the primary without a run-off. Here is how you can help. First, be sure to tell your friends and family across Georgia about Sonny and how important it is to vote in the Republican Primary on August 20 for Sonny. Forward these updates to everyone you know who votes in Georgia. Second, make a financial contribution. You can contribute via the secure web site at www.votesonny.com. You can reply to this e-mail indicating that you would like to make a contribution or you can call Gregg Jones at (229) 435-2285. Third, you can invite someone to go with you to meet Sonny on the 15th. Fourth, you can write a letter to the editor telling why you are voting for Sonny and encouraging others. You probably have far more influence than you realize. Make the best of every opportunity to influence others to lead the way for positive, open, government by electing Sonny Perdue as our next Governor.

Thank you again for all your hard work.

August 7, 2002

Sonny with Darton College Young Republicans
(L-R) Luke Miller, Alison Stephens, Dreau Tucker, Sonny Perdue, Deena
Cheek, Tanika Lakes

Come meet Sonny

Next Thursday, August 15

12:00 Noon - Southwest Georgia Regional Airport

Sonny will be making a campaign stop on August 15 at 12:00 noon at Southwest Georgia Regional Airport. Plan on coming to see Sonny. If you haven't met him in person or if you have friends that haven't met him, this would be a great opportunity. Sonny will be in the meeting room just off the main lobby. There is plenty of parking and the airport will validate your parking ticket so there is no charge.

Dougherty/Lee Sonny Team Gets Positive Squawkbox in Sunday's Albany Herald

Clear evidence of the positive response to Dougherty/Lee Sonny Perdue team's recent telephone campaign came from, of all places, the Squawkbox in the Albany Herald. Much of the time squawkbox comments are of a complaining nature. This one was different:

"I had a call from a Sonny Perdue Campaign worker. He was nice, answered my questions, and didn't even ask me for a donation! That's a first."[23]

Way to go, team!

Sonny Wins Key Endorsements!

The endorsement avalanche is starting to snowball with some big hits from the metro area. The Atlanta Journal Constitution and the Marietta Daily Journal (Bill Byrne's hometown newspaper) have come out strong for Sonny Perdue. The endorsement by the Marietta Daily Journal is huge for Sonny. [24]We are delighted to see these endorsements, especially from the Atlanta area; however, we must remain diligent and committed to gain every vote possible. Endorsements don't cast votes - grassroots voters do, so keep on talking up Sonny and urging people to vote in the Republican Primary for Sonny.

Atlanta Journal Constitution Endorses Perdue in Primary

Calls Him "Serious, Intelligent Public Official"

ATLANTA, GA - The *Atlanta Journal Constitution* - Georgia's largest newspaper and generally not a friend of Republican political candidates - endorsed Sonny Perdue's candidacy in today's edition. The paper called Perdue a "serious, intelligent public official" and said that his "pronouncements are not the babble of a public policy dilettante."

The AJC on Perdue

"...Perdue's 10 years in the Senate, his understanding of how the system works and his ability to fashion constructive legislation would better position him to be effective as governor."

"Perdue also has made several promising proposals to raise ethical standards and root out corruption. He promises to appoint a state inspector general; to overhaul and toughen the state's ethics laws; and to hire outside, independent firms to audit state government departments and agencies."

"Perdue is a serious, intelligent public official whose pronouncements are not the babble of a public policy dilettante. He has begun laying out his ideas in primary debates."

"Though the legislation was not perfect, Perdue's leadership on [natural gas] deregulation and other issues stands in contrast to many Georgia legislators who spend their time dividing the pork or pushing headline-grabbing legislation that clutters the law books without providing meaningful remedies."

"Perdue, former president pro tem of the state Senate, has effectively and responsibly managed complex issues in the legislative arena."[25]

Marietta Daily Journal Endorses Perdue in Primary
Says He "stands head and shoulders above" Byrne and Schrenko

ATLANTA, GA - The Marietta Daily Journal - Cobb County's daily newspaper and Primary opponent Bill Byrne's hometown publication- endorsed Sonny Perdue's candidacy in today's edition. The paper said that Perdue "stands head and shoulders above" Byrne and Linda Schrenko and that Sonny is a "proven believer in lower taxes, cutting government waste and the need for a business-friendly environment."

The MDJ on Perdue

"The story of Perdue's adult life is one of service: service to his country as an Air Force officer and pilot, service to his state and central Georgia as a legislator, and service to his community as a Sunday school teacher, businessman and family man."

"Perdue offers a sharp contrast to his opponents in terms both of experience and temperament."

"In many respects, Georgia's governor can be considered the CEO of a $15 billion a year business. And there's no question as to which of the three Republican hopefuls is best qualified to be at the helm of that business for the next four years: Sonny Perdue."[26]

August 8, 2002

Perdue Announces Plan for "Taxpayer Dividend Act"

Will End Barnes' Era Spending of Surpluses; Require Excess Funds Be Returned or Used to Reduce Debt

ATLANTA, GA - Republican gubernatorial candidate Sonny Perdue today announced his plan to require any future budget surpluses to be spent for debt reduction or tax cuts unless a 2/3 "supermajority" of the Legislature voted for other spending priorities.

"We have to send a message to the Legislature that surpluses belong to the people, not to the government," Perdue told members of the Roswell Rotary Club today. "Roy Barnes and his cronies think surpluses are a slush fund to be spent on their pet pork barrel projects. I believe that, if Georgians have overpaid their taxes, they deserve a refund or corresponding debt reduction."

Perdue also noted that, by spending state budget surpluses, government grows itself and becomes more difficult to cut.

"Spending surpluses of our tax dollars allows government to grow ever larger and makes attempts at cutting its size and scope more difficult," Perdue said. "We must act now to stop this growth before it reaches the point where it is unstoppable."

Details of Perdue's "Taxpayer Dividend Act" are attached.

Taxpayer Dividend Act

Budget surpluses are unnecessary taxes on the people of Georgia, not "free" money for additional state government spending. *Sonny Perdue proposes the "Taxpayers' Dividend Act" - requiring that future surpluses be used to cut taxes or to reduce debt unless there is a bi-partisan 2/3 'supermajority' that can agree on new spending priorities.* This common sense constitutional amendment, which Sonny proposed during his time as a State Senator, has not had a hearing in 3 years under Barnes' administration.

Returning Taxpayer Money

In recent years, Georgia has been fortunate to have annual revenue surpluses [i.] - as much as $1 billion and exceeding $500 million every year during Barnes' administration [ii.]. Despite knowledge of the looming threat of a recession, these surpluses were used to increase government spending, increase the size of state government, and used as pork barrel spending.

Governor Barnes ignored proposals to return this money to taxpayers or pay down the debt. Our total state debt now exceeds $6 billion [iii.]. The $16 billion state budget includes $620 million in interest payments - money that could be spent on education, healthcare or transportation.

Promoting Economic Growth

Perdue's proposal for a supermajority requirement on increased spending is a success in at least a dozen other states. At least fourteen other states have enacted supermajority requirements on spending and taxation. The early evidence from the states with such requirements suggests that they have a restraining influence on the growth of spending - 20 percent less tax revenues and 9 percent less spending in states with supermajority requirements on spending limitations [iv.]. States taking efforts to restrain spending find the added benefit of greater economic growth. Economic growth in supermajority states was 8 percent higher than other states, and job growth was 5 percent higher [v.].[27]

i.   Surpluses are unspent funds at the end of a fiscal year. Surplus funds come from two sources, excess revenue collections over the revenue estimate, and unspent appropriations that were lapsed back to the state treasury and are available for re-appropriation.

ii.   Based on Annual Budget Reports issued by the Governor's Office of Planning and Budget, FY 2000, FY 2001, FY 2002, FY 2003.

iii. The FY 2003 Budget Report summarizes total outstanding debt as of November 30, 2001 to be $5,863,280,000. For FY 2002, Barnes increased bonded indebtedness by $1,347,260,000.

iv.   Differentials in the tax revenue and spending result from the fact that states have revenues streams other than income taxation. Separate studies by Dan Mitchell of the Heritage Foundation and Dean Stansel of the Cato Institute found that taxes and spending grew slower in states with supermajority requirements than in states that did not. Mitchell found that, between 1980 and 1992, tax revenues grew about 20 percent less in supermajority states than in other states, while spending grew 9 percent less.

v.   Stansel's study was broader in scope, examining all tax and spending limitation features-not just supermajority requirements-during the five years preceding and following each state's adoption of fiscal limits. Stansel found that states that adopted tax and spending limits experienced spending growth 0.8 percent higher than the U.S. average before adopting limits, while spending growth was 2.9 percent lower than the average following the adoption of limits.

Come meet Sonny
Next Thursday, August 15
12:00 Noon - Southwest Georgia Regional Airport

Sonny will be making a campaign stop on August 15 at 12:00 noon at Southwest Georgia Regional Airport. Plan on coming to see Sonny. If you haven't met him in person or if you have friends that haven't met him, this would be a great opportunity. Sonny will be in the meeting room just off the main lobby. There is plenty of parking and the airport will validate your parking ticket so there is no charge.

Paid for by Perdue For A New Georgia

August 10, 2002

Sonny with Gregg and Jami Jones' son, Cameron during a visit to Albany

Campaigning the Old Fashioned Way:
Kissing One Baby at a Time

Come meet Sonny

Thursday, August 15

12:00 Noon - Southwest Georgia Regional Airport

Sonny will be making a campaign stop on August 15 at 12:00 noon at Southwest Georgia Regional Airport. Plan on coming to see Sonny. If you haven't met him in person or if you have friends that haven't met him, this would be a great opportunity. Sonny will be in the meeting room just off the main lobby. There is plenty of parking and the airport will validate your parking ticket so there is no charge.

And Another Endorsement!
Savannah Morning News Endorses Perdue

4th Major Newspaper Endorsement Says Sonny has "Most to Offer in Terms of Experience, Knowledge and Temperament"

SAVANNAH, GA - **The Savannah Morning News** became the latest major newspaper to endorse Sonny Perdue in Georgia's GOP Gubernatorial Primary. Saying he "has the most to offer in terms of experience, knowledge and temperament" and "a good blend of legislative, leadership and business experience." This week, the **Atlanta Journal-Constitution**, **Marietta Daily Journal** and the alternative weekly **Creative Loafing** all also endorsed Perdue. Perdue's opponents have received no media endorsements.[28]

On Perdue:

"State Sen. Sonny Perdue has the most to offer in terms of experience, knowledge and temperament. Voters can expect him to engage Mr. Barnes in healthy debate about Georgia's future."

"Mr. Perdue has a good blend of legislative, leadership and business experience. He knows what's important to Georgia and has proposed some worthy ideas about how to improve state government."

"Mr. Perdue, 55, who runs an agri-business company in Bonaire, is a man who puts principles over power. Even when it costs him. He served in the legislature for 10 years, most of that time as a

Democrat. He earned the respect of his peers and rose to serve as president pro tem of the Senate -- until he switched parties and became a Republican in 1998."

"Mr. Perdue has shown that he takes public policy seriously. He's no political pretender. He understands how government affects people's lives -- for better or worse."

On Byrne and Schrenko:

"The other Republican candidates, State Superintendent of Schools Linda Schrenko and former Cobb County Commission Chairman Bill Byrne, have political and management experience. But Ms. Schrenko's record is spotty. And while Mr. Byrne has gotten high marks for improving Cobb County government, leading a county commission is not the same as getting things done in the Georgia Legislature. Mr. Perdue outpoints him on his knowledge of the system. He knows where the problems are and what needs to be done to fix them."[29]

Good Reason to Vote Republican August 20

With all the local races in Dougherty County being in the Democratic Primary, one may wonder what good reason someone would have to vote in the Republican Primary. You have heard the old saying "All politics is local." The following letter to People's Forum in the Albany Herald offers good reasoning for voting in the Republican Primary. Spread the word around - Vote Republican, Vote Sonny!

People's Forum - Albany Herald - Thursday, August 8, 2002

GOP candidates best for protecting MCLB

"All politics is local." Dougherty County voters have the opportunity to cast a ballot in the upcoming primary for candidates who will have a direct impact on the largest employer in our area by asking for a Republican ballot and voting for Saxby Chambliss for U.S. senator and Sonny Perdue for governor.

The Marine Corps Logistics Base-Albany has been referred to as the economic hub of Southwest Georgia. Saxby Chambliss has been an avid supporter of MCLB-Albany and has close ties with President Bush. Sonny Perdue is from Houston County, home of Warner Robins Air Force Base and former Sen. Sam Nunn. Sonny also has close ties with President Bush and played a key role in defending Georgia military bases during the last round of base closings.

Do not assume that statewide Republican candidates in the primary do not need your vote. All races are expected to be close. MCLB-Albany could lose two valuable friends, Saxby and Sonny, in the Republican primary because Dougherty County voters overlooked the influence of these two men on our local economy.

The presidential election in Florida should be a sobering reminder that every vote counts. Make your vote count for the hub of our economy by asking for a Republican ballot and voting for Saxby Chambliss for U.S. senator and Sonny Perdue for governor.[30]

DONALD E. COLE
Albany

August 13, 2002

Come meet Sonny
Thursday, August 15
12:00 Noon - Southwest Georgia Regional Airport

August 15, 2002

Sonny Arrives Today!
Thursday, August 15
12:00 Noon - Southwest Georgia Regional Airport

Sonny will be making a campaign stop on Thursday, August 15 at 12:00 noon at Southwest Georgia Regional Airport. Plan on coming to see Sonny. If you haven't met him in person or if you have friends that haven't met him, this would be a great opportunity. Sonny will be in the meeting room just off the main lobby. There is plenty of parking and the airport will validate your parking ticket so there is no charge.

August 16, 2002

Great Crowd Meets Sonny in Albany!

Sonny Perdue arrived in Albany at noon today, greeted by a crowd of enthusiastic supporters at the Southwest Georgia Regional Airport. Some long-time Southwest Georgia political watchers said that this was the largest crowd to meet a candidate at the airport including candidates such as Paul Coverdell. Sonny is on a statewide campaign final sprint to a primary election victory!

Albany Herald Endorses Sonny!

In addition to the enthusiastic crowd, Sonny received another key endorsement from the Albany Herald. It was a great welcome on another visit to Albany and Southwest Georgia. More to follow on the Herald Endorsement.

Sonny to Visit Valdosta

Come meet Sonny Perdue on the 19th in Valdosta from 9:30 to 10:30 at the Crescent on Patterson Street. Contact Bill Fuqua by e-mail: fuquab@surfsouth.com, at his office 229-242-2225, or home 229-559-4999 for directions or more information.

During these last days before the Primary, Sonny Perdue is the one Republican Candidate proving that he is for all of Georgia by investing his time all across the state, not just in the Metro Atlanta Area.

Blue Ballot Barbeque in Moultrie August 19

The Colquitt County Republican Party invites you to join Saxby and Julianne Chambliss and Congressman Jack Kingston for a FREE evening of fun and entertainment for the whole family. Enjoy the Blue Ballot Barbeque Monday, August 19th, at 6:30 p.m. Sunbelt Expo Livestock Pavilion, rain or shine. On Tuesday, August 20th support Sonny and the Republican Party by asking for the Blue Ballot.

August 16, 2002

Barnes Launches Attack Ads on Sonny

WALB TV in Albany as well as other stations across the state just ran a Barnes TV spot attacking Sonny Perdue specifically. The attacks are a Willie Horton type of advertisement. Governor Barnes is spending heavily buying TV time in markets across the state to run these ads. Sonny held a press conference with WSB TV in Atlanta firing back at Barnes pointing out the irony of a trial lawyer who spent a career trying to set criminals free criticizing Sonny's record.

Searching for Willie Horton, Finding Elliot Ness

Roy Barnes has gone looking for his own Willie Horton claiming that Sonny sought preferential treatment for criminals.

Fact: Like virtually every Georgia State Senator and Representative, Sonny passed along requests from constituents regarding family members who were incarcerated. In no case were recommendations made by the Senator or his staff - the requests were merely forwarded to the appropriate authorities to act on as they saw fit. Not one single call or letter urged action on the part of the Pardons and Parole Board.

The requests were typically from relatives (mostly mothers and grandmothers) who were too aged or infirm to travel long distances to visit their incarcerated kin and wanted them moved to a prison closer to home. The Pardons and Parole Board told inquiring reporters that these actions were entirely appropriate and routine.

Sonny's anti-crime record is impeccable. Sonny twice sponsored bills requiring all violent felons to serve at least 90% of their terms before the Pardons and Parole Board could even consider releasing them. He also championed legislation to stiffen the penalties for crimes against police officers, firefighters, EMTs, and other public safety officials. Sonny even authored a bill to abolish the State Board of Pardons and Paroles in 1998.[31]

August 21, 2002

Sonny's Grass Roots Wins Without Run-Off

Sonny has clinched the Republican Nomination for Governor with a majority. The race for the Governor's Mansion is on its way and, as Sonny said last Thursday here in Albany, he is ready to go after Roy Barnes. This win in a three-way race without a run-off is a tribute to Sonny's grass roots campaign that is organized across Georgia. You made this happen, and you will make it happen again in November.

A Message from the Voters Who Know Sonny

Looking at numbers across the state, the people of Houston County sent a crystal clear message about their respect and support for Sonny. Sonny received over 93% of the vote (11,628 out of 12,500) from the people who know him. This is a phenomenal turn out and show of support. Just meet Sonny and you will understand why the people who know him support him in such an overwhelming way.

A Great Letter to the Editor

The Albany Herald published Beth Hall's letter to the editor in Monday's paper. She summed up well why people voted for Sonny and why Sonny will be our next Governor.

People's Forum - Albany Herald – Monday, August 19, 2002

Perdue has vision to lead as governor

"If my people, which are called by my name, shall humble themselves, and pray, and seek my face, and turn from their wicked ways, then will I hear from heaven, and will forgive their sin, and will heal their land." 2 Chronicles 7:14.

Grassroots: Leading Others to Accomplish the Impossible

Sonny Perdue, Republican nominee for governor of Georgia, is just that: a humble man of moral value with a family oriented way of life. A trustworthy man faithful to God first, family and those who support him to stand for what is right and honorable.

A new day is dawning in Georgia and in the arena of diplomacy in our great country. Our founding fathers were faith-based men that built our nation on, "In God we trust." Isn't it time we return to our heritage and values of our forefathers and elect men who are motivated and driven by their faith, guided by integrity and live with a code of morals that have no fear of the price to pay.

Sonny Perdue knows this all too well by sacrificing his position in the Democratic Party by turning Republican. This was due to his desire to return power back to the people, dismantle corrupt politics and create a local empowerment of stimulated education for future generations.

Helen Keller, blind from birth, wrote, "To have eyes and no vision would be worst than being blind." Elect Sonny Perdue, a man with a vision in favor of the people.[32]

BETH HALL
Albany

August 21, 2002

Sonny Returns to Albany Tomorrow
Thursday August 22, 2002

10:45 AM Veteran's Park Amphitheater

Sonny Perdue and Saxby Chambliss will hold a rally from 10:45 - 11:00 am tomorrow at the Veteran's Park Amphitheater across from the James Gray Civic Center. Come join the crowd to kick off the General Election campaign for our next Governor and U.S. Senator. We had a wonderful crowd last Thursday at the Airport; make this one an even larger crowd.

To demoralized educators and gerrymandered Georgians, Sonny and Saxby have the same message that Dick Cheney sent the U.S. Military at the Republican National Convention in 2000, "Help is on the way."

Let's let Albany and Southwest Georgia lead the charge to take Georgia back for the people. History is being made right here in Albany. Bring your friends and family to be a part of history.

August 22, 2002

You helped make the Primary campaign a resounding success. Sonny asked us to pass on his thanks. The campaign is now underway. Sonny and Saxby held a great joint rally in Albany. This was the first joint event for them in the General Election campaign and we are proud that it was held right here in Albany. An update on the rally will be coming. Thank you again for all your help. We look forward to working with each one of you to elect Sonny as the first Republican Governor of Georgia in 130 years.

Mary and I want to take this opportunity to thank you for your hard work and support for our campaign. Our huge victory on Tuesday was due to your efforts in getting our message out to the people across Georgia.

Now the people have spoken and told us that they are ready for a government of the people, by the people and for the people. They are ready for change.

But there is no rest for the weary. We still have much to do and we need your help now more than in the Primary.

If you would like to help us financially, please click here.

If you would like to get involved in the campaign in other ways, please click here.

Again, thank you for your support. And remember to vote in the General Election on November 5th.

August 23, 2002

Georgia House Minority Leader, Lynn Westmoreland introduces
Saxby and Julianne Chambliss, Sonny Perdue, and Nancy Coverdell

Sonny and Saxby Hold Joint Rally in Albany!

Sonny Perdue and Saxby Chambliss kicked off the first of many joint campaign rallies across the state of Georgia yesterday as they marched toward the Governor's mansion and the Senate floor. Sonny summed up the message of their campaigns when he said, "Georgians have been conservative voters with conservative principles and values. And we represent those values... of lower taxes and less government, conservative fiscal and social values that we can stand for. That's what Georgians want and that's what we're going to bring to them."

Albany and Southwest Georgia can be proud that Sonny and Saxby chose Albany as the place to begin their united march to victory.

WALB TV Jim Wallace reported:

"The party has nominated two strong candidates to run for U.S. Senate and Governor. Senatorial candidate Saxby Chambliss of Moultrie, and Gubernatorial candidate Sonny Perdue made campaign stops in Albany Thursday. They are working together to break the Democratic strong hold on the state. With cheers in the background, Republican Senatorial Candidate Saxby Chambliss and Republican Gubernatorial Candidate Sonny Perdue, walked down the steps of the Albany Veterans Park Amphitheater. A group of Southwest Georgia Republicans and school children were there to greet them."[33]

August 31, 2002

Two Reasons Sonny Perdue is Running for Governor

Dougherty/Lee Steering Committee Meeting
Coming Soon

The Dougherty/Lee Chairs are planning for a Dougherty/Lee Steering Committee meeting soon. We had a great grassroots victory across Georgia in the Primary. We have to step up our efforts now for the General Election in November. Excitement for Sonny is growing rapidly. If you want to help Sonny in any way over these next two months, we want to hear from you. Reply to this e-mail and let us know how we can contact you with details on the steering committee meeting.

Sonny Fund Raiser in Dougherty Coming Soon

Another Fund Raiser for Sonny in Dougherty County is in the planning stages right now. The target date is October 10. If you are interested in being a part of this fund-raiser, reply to this e-mail or call Gregg Jones at (229) 435-2285.

Labor Day Weekend

Labor Day weekend 2002 brings with it a new set of feelings as we enter into the month of September and are reminded of the evil terrorist attack on our nation one year ago. This Labor Day our nation is at war.

Our President, Cabinet, members of Congress, Armed Forces, and the American people enter into this month with a resolve to defeat and eliminate those who seek to harm our fellow Americans. Our cause is a just and righteous cause. Pause during this Labor Day Weekend to pray for President Bush and ask for God's guidance, strength, and firm reliance on His control and protection.

September 6, 2002

Across the Generations - People Love Sonny!

Report on Statewide Grassroots Virtual Conference

Sixty days before the primary, Sonny Perdue used state of the art technology to hold a conference where he told supporters across the state that we could win the primary without a run-off. Pundits scoffed, pollsters laughed, but the grassroots team went to work and did the impossible. Last night, about sixty days before the general election, Sonny again pulled together county chairs from across the state in a virtual conference room to communicate the vision and plan for victory on November 5. We will do it again.

Sonny's grassroots team continues to spread its roots and sprout new supporters from all walks of life and across party lines. Southwest Georgia is a key part of Sonny's plan to win. You all have done a fantastic job talking up Sonny and we can see the evidence. Keep on telling your friends and neighbors as the Sonny Perdue grassroots keeps on spreading and sinking its roots. You are part of an historic election campaign that will impact generations to come.

Fund Raiser for Sonny in Albany October 10

Sonny will be in Albany on October 10 for a fund-raiser at the home of Jack and Dotty Jones. Gregg Jones has over 20 host couples committed. The cost of the event is $150.00 per person. We are expecting a huge crowd to meet and mingle with Sonny. Sonny's schedule is packed and this may be the best time to visit with him in our area. For more information, just reply to this e-mail or give Gregg Jones a call at 229-435-2285.

September 13, 2002

Rolling Up Our Sleeves and Back to Work

The Primary and run-offs are over and the Sonny machine is rolling again. The phone banks will start up Monday to continue to build the e-mail update list and secure permissions for yard signs. September 28 will be a big day of distributing campaign materials statewide. Sonny's grassroots team grows every day.

The Power of Your Influence

Never underestimate the power of your personal influence. You have a circle of family and friends who will vote for Sonny simply because you tell them that you are voting for him. One of the best things you can do is forward these updates to your friends and put a little personal note at the beginning and in the subject line so they will know that it isn't spam. Sonny's campaign is grassroots and your personal e-mail to people you know is one sure way to spread those grassroots. If you forward an e-mail to 5 people and each one of those forwards to 5 people, the sphere of influence spreads like a wildfire. 5 who send to 5 who send to 5 who send to 5 will generate a total of 780 voters influenced for Sonny. These updates are going out at least once each week. If you have a friend who lives anywhere in Georgia or who knows others who live in Georgia, then send it out and write a personal update on your family while you are at it. It's a great way to keep in touch and to keep those grassroots spreading.

Making a Sacrifice to Return Power to the People

Another fundraiser for Sonny is scheduled for October 10 at the home of Jack and Dotty Jones. Roy Barnes has millions in his war chest. Sonny can't match him dollar for dollar, but he does need to raise a substantial sum in order to buy the much-needed TV time in the last days before the election. The fundraiser is asking $150.00 per person as an investment in the power of the people over the people of power. Roy Barnes has raised his money primarily from out-of-state and big corporations. Sonny's funds are coming primarily from people just like you who are making a personal sacrifice to return the power to the people. Many of you reading this update have probably never contributed to a political campaign. This election will be won because thousands, just like you, will do something you have never done before. You will write a check, not as a mere contribution, but as an investment. A multi-billion dollar corporation can write a check for $10,000 and not blink an eye. But when you write a check for $150.00, you shed tears. It isn't just money to you, it is your heart, your soul, your courageous stand like David against Goliath. As far as the bank ledger goes, money is money. But when you make the investment that represents your toil and labor, something happens that can't be measured on a bank ledger.

The final words of the Declaration of Independence are an example of meager resources invested in faith in a just and righteous cause. $150.00 doesn't seem like much when compared to the price paid by the early Americans to establish our nation. Read the words slowly and let them sink in to your mind and heart. "And for the support of this Declaration, with a firm reliance on the protection of divine Providence, we mutually pledge to each other our Lives, our Fortunes and our sacred

Honor." This campaign is simple. It is about the people of power versus the power of the people. Make your investment. Reply to this e-mail and say that you want to join the ranks of the people who are investing to return power to the people.

September 20, 2002

Hey! Look! Look! Look!

Tuesday September 24th 6:30 PM

Blackbeard's Restaurant

2209 N Slappey Blvd. Albany

Come join Chris Young from Sonny's State Campaign Office on Tuesday night at Blackbeard's to see the Victory 2002 plan for Sonny's campaign. Chris has some exciting numbers and analysis to share. This is a great opportunity to meet Sonny supporters and see the big picture of Sonny's history-making campaign. Don Cole, Dougherty County Chairman will present the plan for the Dougherty/Lee County effort. This is not a fundraiser. You only pay for the meal you eat.

September 23, 2002

Hard working volunteer, Jon Ayres

Signs Going Up Soon!

Our team has been adding names to the list of those who want yard signs and they will be going up soon. If you want a sign in your yard, or if you need a new sign, please respond to this e-mail or call Gregg Jones at (229) 435-2285. Our phone volunteers have been calling people across Dougherty and Lee, and the number of people wanting signs is phenomenal. We are recruiting new volunteers to meet the demand. Invest a couple of hours one evening to help deliver the signs. You can be a part. Just reply to this e-mail or call Gregg Jones to let him know that you want to help and we'll give you more details.

Reminder
Blackbeards 6:30 pm Tuesday September 24

Come join Chris Young from Sonny's State Campaign Office on Tuesday night at Blackbeard's to see the Victory 2002 plan for Sonny's campaign. Chris has some exciting numbers and analysis to share. This is a great opportunity to meet Sonny supporters and see the big picture of Sonny's history-making campaign. Don Cole, Dougherty County Chairman will present the plan for the

Dougherty/Lee County effort. This is not a fundraiser. You only pay for the meal you eat.

Fund Raiser for Sonny in Albany October 10

Call Gregg Jones at (229) 435-2285 for details

September 26, 2002

Crowd Gathers in Albany to
Hear Report on Campaign

Chris Young from Sonny's staff gave a positive report on trends to a crowd of approximately 40 Sonny supporters at Blackbeard's Restaurant in Albany last Tuesday. Don Cole, Dougherty Committee Co-Chair, followed with a plan of action for Dougherty and Lee Counties. Significant facts from the presentation:

- More people asked for a Republican ballot across the state than asked for a Democratic ballot.
- Sonny won in 19 of 20 Metro Atlanta counties.
- In 1998 Metro Atlanta represented 62% of the GOP Primary Vote in 2002 it represented only 55%.
- 37 Counties doubled the number of Republican votes from 1998.

- Republican votes increased in 131 counties since 1998 while Democratic votes decreased in 141 counties.
- In 1998 Paul Coverdell won 70 counties, which also went for Roy Barnes.
- In the primary Sonny won those 70 counties by an average of 67% and GOP ballots outnumbered Democratic ballots by 16%.

Sonny's campaign strategy has focused on the group known as the "Coverdell Coalition." These are the conservative voters who tend to vote independently based on the values of the candidate and live in the non-metro areas. A key factor to keep in mind is that in many of these 70 counties, there were important local races on the Democratic ballot. This shows that, in many cases, the people who voted in the Republican primary voted out of a strong desire to vote for Sonny Perdue. They gave up an opportunity to vote in a local race because they wanted to invest their vote in Sonny for Governor. Chris shared that in some of the counties there were reports of voters in the Democratic primary marking through Roy Barnes on the ballot and writing in Sonny Perdue.

The crowd at Blackbeard's was positive and enthusiastic for Sonny and other Republican candidates as well. Debbie Cannon represented Saxby Chambliss at the meeting. Ed Rynders, candidate for State House, and Bill Farnsworth, candidate for Dougherty County Commission, were also in attendance. We are moving forward to win.

Fund Raiser for Sonny in Albany October 10

Call Gregg Jones at (229) 435-2285 for details

October 1, 2002

President Bush Coming to Georgia to Endorse Sonny!

Are you a little weary of seeing all these Democratic candidates with references to President Bush in their commercials? President Bush is about to set the record straight. He comes to Georgia on October 17 for a Republican Unity Rally and will endorse Sonny Perdue as our next Governor. It is really simple. If you want to help President Bush, then vote Republican.

Dougherty/Lee Campaign Kick-Off

Left to Right - Jackson Murphy, Gregg Jones, Don Cole, Dreau Tucker, Bruce Lambert, Alane Marks, Robin Brown, Joe Woody, Eric Newman, Abigail Smith, Gary Smith, Caleb Smith, David Maschke, Beth Hall

With 5 weeks to go before Sonny is elected as our next Governor, the Dougherty/Lee Sonny Perdue team kicked off the General Election campaign drive by placing over 150 yard signs in one afternoon. The demand for yard signs is running high. Sonny's sign campaign is unlike many other sign campaigns. First, all the people working to put out signs are volunteers - investing their time in the worthy cause to elect Sonny Perdue as our next Governor. Second, yard signs were placed on private property and only in those locations where the owners had asked for a Perdue yard sign. A Sonny Perdue sign represents a grassroots commitment for Sonny Perdue.

Sonny Coming to Albany October 10!

Sonny will be in Albany on October 10 for a fundraiser at the home of Jack and Dotty Jones. Cost is $150.00 per person. Call Gregg Jones at Albany Travel 229-435-2285 if you would like to attend. Sonny will also be cutting the ribbon for the Republican Headquarters. Watch for updates.

Saxby Signs Available

Sonny's campaign team is united with other Republican candidates to spread the word and get out the vote. Saxby Chambliss signs are available at the office of Gary Smith. Gary is the Dougherty County Republican Party Chairman. Gary can also give you more information and help connect you to ways to help in other campaigns. Ed Rynders for State House, Carden Summers for State Senate, Doug Everett for Public Service Commission, and Bill Farnsworth for Dougherty County Commission are all candidates with districts in Dougherty County. Give Gary a call at 434-1960 and ask how you can help.

Get a Great Deal on a New Pair of Boots

www.bootbarnes.com

October 4, 2002

Jackson Murphy - Left and Dreau Tucker placing signs
and distributing information in Lake Park area

Everywhere You Look, It's Sonny Country!

Signs continue to go up all over Dougherty and Lee County. The response is somewhat overwhelming. We hate to have to start rationing signs so we will keep finding a way to get signs to everyone who wants one. While the team was placing these signs people would stop and ask to have a sign at their house. One lady driving through the area stopped her car and asked to have a Sonny bumper sticker placed on it right then and there. She also asked to have a sign placed at her home in another area of town. Sonny is even ahead of hometown Mark Taylor in the sign count and that's even counting all the Taylor signs stuck in right-of-ways. Sonny signs represent Sonny votes. You can't say that about all the others.

Sonny/Roy Debate Tuesday in Perry at Georgia National Fair

Joe Cornelius of Sonny's Warner Robins Office Issues Call to Arms

Next Tuesday, October 8th, there will be a debate between Sonny and Roy. It will be in Reeves Arena at the Georgia National Fairgrounds in Perry (call Joe if you need directions). The doors open at 5:30 and the seating is on a first-come first-serve basis. There are 8500 seats in Reeves and I want EVERY ONE OF THEM FILLED WITH A SONNY SUPPORTER. Cost of admission to the fair is $6, but admissions to the debate is free and open to the general public.

Here are the rules for the debate:

- Signs ARE allowed
- Lapel Stickers ARE allowed
- T-Shirts ARE allowed

This is the first of three debates and the ONLY one not in Atlanta. This debate is in Houston County and I want Roy Barnes to regret he ever left West Paces Ferry Road.

Folks, I need your help on this one. All of the media from Atlanta will be here to cover this event. I want that arena to be FILLED with people wearing Sonny t-shirts, holding signs and chanting "SONNY! SONNY! SONNY!"

Bring your wife, your husband, your children, your neighbors, your friends, your coworkers, your church, and most importantly, bring your Sonny Shirt and Sonny Sign.

We will not have this type of opportunity again. Please forward this to your contact list and call all of your friends and family and get them to the debate next week!

Please call me here at the office if you have any questions.[34]

For a Better Georgia,

Joe Cornelius III, Perdue For a New Georgia
Warner Robins Office - 478-929-4332

Perdue Camp Puts Barnes Ads on Own Website - Desperate Barnes Attacks

After determining that $10 million in TV commercials have significantly helped his candidacy, Sonny's campaign decided to put Roy Barnes' ads on his own website to assure even wider viewership.

"Despite their below-average quality, Barnes' ads have had quite an impact due to the sheer volume of them clogging the airwaves," said Perdue spokesman Dan McLagan. "The education ads have infuriated the teachers Roy blamed for his education failures as well as parents lamenting Georgia's abysmal SAT scores. The vegetable stand ads failed to spark interest in the Governor's doubtless fascinating life history. Even the ad attacking Sonny before the Primary backfired."[35]

Barnes' Attacks Sonny on HOPE - Sonny Shoots Straight

Roy Barnes spent $10 million on an ineffective effort to get Georgians to like him. His numbers are not moving because the voters of this state aren't buying his snake oil. He's stuck at 45%, so he did what we predicted. He went negative and his ad is a lie.

One of two new Barnes ads rips Perdue for voting as a state senator "again and again" to oppose the lottery-funded scholarship program, which pays college tuition for students who earn and keep a "B" average.

The Facts:

- Sonny actually CO-SPONSORED the resolution in 1998 (SR 529) that would permanently protect the HOPE Scholarship. His resolution stated that lottery funds had to be used first and foremost for the funding of HOPE Scholarships. This resolution was adopted by the General Assembly and eventually passed by the people of Georgia in November.

- Sonny voted YES on the vote to allow a statewide referendum on the lottery (HR 7 in 1991). He believed that the people of Georgia should have their voice heard on this issue.

- • Sonny was Chairman of the Higher Education Committee in 1993 when the first HOPE scholarships were being awarded.

This attack is a fundamental shift in the campaign. Roy Barnes' failed agenda has not worked, so he is resorting to a negative campaign attack on Sonny. It was a fight that we knew was coming and one that we welcome. Sonny Perdue has a strong record of public service and if the governor wants to hit us there, then bring it on.[36]

October 17, 2002

www.sowegavotesonny.com

Southwest Georgia is on the cutting edge with its own web site focusing on Sonny's campaign in our neck of the woods. Check on the link above. If you have any news or updates on Sonny events in your area, send them to victory@sowegavotesonny.com. Sonny knows the needs and interests of Southwest Georgians. Forward this link to your friends.

Sonny Coming to Albany October 10

Sonny will be coming to Albany on October 10 for a fundraiser at the home of Jack and Dotty Jones. If you are interested in attending, reply to this e-mail or give Gregg Jones a call at 229-435-2285. More updates to follow and will also be posted on www.sowegavotesonny.com.

October 8, 2002

Come Join Sonny at Rally in Albany
Thursday, October 10, 2002 5:30 PM
Albany Travel Agency 2305 Dawson Road

Sonny Perdue will hold a press conference and rally in Albany at 5:30 pm on Thursday, October 10, 2002 at Albany Travel Agency, 2305 Dawson Road. (Next to the old location of Gus's BBQ, across from Phoebe Northwest). Come meet Sonny in person and show your support for our next Governor. Sonny will be commenting on small businesses and the endorsement he received from the National Federation of Independent Business (NFIB).

The **National Federation of Independent Business (NFIB)** is Georgia's largest small-business advocacy group, with 10,000 members statewide. A non-profit, non-partisan organization founded in 1943, NFIB represents the consensus views of its 600,000 members to lawmakers in Washington, D.C., and all 50 state capitals. For more information on NFIB and small-business issues, visit the NFIB web site at www.nfib.com.

Call Gregg Jones at 229-435-2285 for details
on the rally and the fund-raiser.

See You There!

October 10, 2002

Sonny at Rally Today in Albany
Thursday, October 10, 2002 5:30 PM
Albany Travel Agency 2305 Dawson Road

Come meet our next Governor, Sonny Perdue at a press conference and rally in Albany at 5:30 pm today, Thursday, October 10, 2002 at Albany Travel Agency, 2305 Dawson Road. (Next to the old location of Gus's BBQ, across from Phoebe Northwest). Come meet Sonny in person and show your support for our next Governor. Sonny will be commenting on small businesses and the endorsement he received from the National Federation of Independent Business (NFIB).

The National Federation of Independent Business (NFIB) is Georgia's largest small-business advocacy group, with 10,000 members statewide. A non-profit, non-partisan organization founded in 1943, NFIB represents the consensus views of its 600,000 members to lawmakers in Washington, D.C., and all 50 state capitals. For more information on NFIB and small-business issues, visit the NFIB web site at www.nfib.com.

Call Gregg Jones at 229-435-2285 for details
on the rally and the fund-raiser.

See You There!

October 13, 2002

Southwest Georgia Gives
Sonny's Campaign $60,000!

A large enthusiastic crowd met Sonny Perdue for a press conference on Thursday in front of Albany Travel on Dawson Road. Thousands of vehicles passed by during the rush hour waving and honking at the crowd gathered to greet Sonny Perdue on his visit to Albany. Sonny took the opportunity to comment on the endorsement of the National Federation of Independent Business he just received. NFIB Georgia members were recently asked in a member survey to determine whether the non-partisan small-business advocacy group should get involved in the gubernatorial race. The results of the survey were 95 percent in favor of doing so, and 88 percent were for supporting Sonny Perdue.

Later that evening, cars were backed up hundreds of feet down West Doublegate Drive in Albany near the home of Jack and Dotty Jones where supporters added $60,000 to Sonny Perdue's campaign fund. The crowd cheered and applauded as Gregg Jones announced the preliminary total. Sonny said that he was so proud of the support he was receiving from Southwest Georgia. Identifying with the agricultural interests of Southwest Georgia Sonny said, "After 130 years of Democratic rule, it's time to rotate the crops, and clean out the Barnes."

Perdue Unveils "HOPE Chest" Plan To Protect Scholarship Fund

Reminds Georgians Of Barnes' Anti-Lottery, Anti-HOPE Run

KENNESAW, GA - During a visit with a group of AP Government students at North Cobb High School, Republican Gubernatorial Candidate Sonny Perdue announced his plan to create a "HOPE Chest" investment reserve to ensure that the HOPE scholarship program would be protected and strengthened under his administration. Perdue went on to unveil his plan for the HOPE Chest program.

"I will propose a constitutional amendment that will ensure that HOPE scholarship assistance and Pre-Kindergarten programs are the only annual expenditures allowed with Lottery Revenues," Perdue said. "All excess revenues will be trusted and will grow in an endowment for future generations. While Roy Barnes is borrowing against our children's future, the Perdue Administration will invest in it."

Afterwards, Perdue reminded reporters that Roy Barnes was the chief opponent of the lottery during his failed 1990 run for Governor.

Armed with a list of newspaper excerpts, Perdue said, "I supported a referendum on the lottery while he was campaigning against the people even having a choice." Perdue added, "If Roy Barnes had been successful in his 1990 gubernatorial campaign, the HOPE scholarship would not exist."

Perdue also noted that as a the gubernatorial candidate Roy Barnes called the lottery an "irresponsible campaign gimmick" and said that it was misleading the voters to imply that it would make a serious difference in financing education. [37]

October 16, 2002

Sonny Returns to Albany Next Friday
October 25, 5:00 pm Veteran's Park

Sonny will be returning to Albany on Friday, October 25th for a rally at Veteran's Park at 5:00 pm. Come out to meet Sonny in person and bring a friend. He wants to personally meet as many people from Southwest Georgia as possible in his final tour around the state before he is elected as our next Governor.

Georgia Veterans Line-Up Behind Perdue; Decry Barnes' Failure on Military Ballots

One of Nation's Most Decorated Living Veteran To Lead Perdue's Efforts

ABBEVILLE, GA - In front of a veterans memorial and flanked by veterans from across middle Georgia, Sonny Perdue denounced the failure of Georgia officials to distribute absentee ballots to military personnel in a timely manner as required by state law.

"It is a travesty that the men and women who are serving our nation and fighting the War on Terrorism may be disenfranchised by the state of Georgia," said Perdue before a crowd of supporters who gathered at the Wilcox County Courthouse.

Perdue also announced that General Ray Davis, one of America's most decorated living veterans, today endorsed his bid for Governor. General Davis, who received the Medal of Honor, the Navy Cross, and the Distinguished Medal of Service, will lead Perdue's statewide Veterans Coalition.

"I could not be more proud that General Davis has agreed to lead my Veterans Coalition. General Davis is a true American hero, and exemplifies the values Georgian's hold most dear," said Perdue.

Davis is joined by over 250 veterans from all corners of the state who have already signed-up to join the Perdue team.

"I am running for Governor to return honesty, integrity, and leadership to Georgia: the values I learned while serving my country in the United States Air Force. I could not be more proud that General Davis and so many veterans from across Georgia have joined our team," said Perdue.

In the past weeks, revelations surfaced that thousands of Georgia's active duty military personnel may be unable to cast their votes in the November general election. Absentee ballots, which by law must be printed and ready for distribution 45 days prior to the election, have yet to be printed. Georgia law requires ballots to be in the Election Office by 7pm on Election Day, with no provision for when the ballot is postmarked. Mail service for servicemen aboard ship or stationed overseas is notoriously slow, meaning they may be unable to vote in November.

"It is time for a Governor who honors and respects our military personnel, rather than disenfranchising the very people fighting for our liberties in the War on Terrorism," said Perdue.

Perdue has reached out to the families of those serving their nation, championing their push to have all legally cast votes from military personnel counted.

"Our servicemen are putting their lives on hold, and putting their lives on the line, to defend our freedoms. To take away their right to vote while they are fighting the War on Terrorism is the ultimate insult and betrayal," said Cynthia Ivey, whose husband, Master Sergeant Gary Ivey, is currently serving in the 1st Special Forces Battalion, 20th Special Forces Group in an undisclosed location somewhere outside the continental United States.[38]

Sonny Veteran County Chairs and Supporters

Appling County
Larry Stone, United States Army
Atkinson County
Charles Lockwood, United States Army
Bacon County
Johnny "Bucky" Hayes, United States Army
W.E. Miller, United States Air Force
Baker County
Mike Lanier, United States Navy
Baldwin County
Jackson Cox, United States Army

Barrow County
Gerald Moon, United States Navy
Ken Thompson, United States Army
Bartow County
Dean Glidewell, United States Army
Ben Hill County
D. Eastridge, United States Army
Berrien County
Jimmy Knowles, United States Army
Bibb County
Dutch McLendon, Unites States Army
Brantley County
Anthony Barber, United States Army
Clyde Aldridge, United States Army
Dennis Watkins, United States Air Force
Stephanie Watkins, United States Army
Bryan County
Walter Meeks, United States Navy
Butts County
William Smith, United States Army
Camden County
Stephen Raley, United States Navy
Candler County
Ralph Hanson, United States Navy
Carroll County
John Langley, United States Army
Catoosa County
Bill Clark, United States Army
Charlton County
Bud Morris, Jr., United States Army

Chatham County
Bill Browning, United States Navy
Dan Fogarty, United States Army
Henry Kennedy, Georgia National Guard
Jack McCall, United States Army
Chattooga County
Robby Eversole, United States Army
Cherokee County
Rick Bobbitt, United States Air Force
Bart Brannon, United States Army
Dick Hall, United States Army
Clarke County
Bob Gregory, United States Navy
Clayton County
John Morris, United States Army
Vernon Hayes, United States Army
Clinch County
R.A. Holmes, United States Navy
Cobb County
Thomas Bruce, United States Air Force
Ira McKee, United States Air Force
Coffee County
Harvey Adams, United States Air Force
Herman Adams, United States Army
Homer Adams, United States Navy
Frank Anderson, United States Coast Guard
Jim Anderson, United States Air Force
Wilbert Anderson, United States Air Force
Simon Atkinson, United States Army
Herbert Batten, United States Army
James D. Brown, Sr., United States Navy
James D. Brown, Jr., United States Navy

Tom Buckner, United States Marines
Bob Carmichael, United States Army
Buster Carmichael, United States Army
Clarence Carter, United States Army
Harry Carver, United States Army
Donny Courson, United States Army
Kathy Courson, United States Army
Herbert Davis, United States Navy
Mack Davis, United States Navy
Aubrey Fallin, United States Marines
Jesse Goodman, United States Air Force
Fernell Harkeroad, United States Air Force
Dewey Hayes, United States Army
Lee Henderson, United States Coast Guard
Gene Holdon, United States Army
Ricky Lott, United States Army
Herbert Meeks, United States Navy
W.L. Meeks, United States Navy
Richard Meeks, United States Marines
R.O. Mitchel, United States Army
James Moore, United States Air Force
Robert Morgan, United States Army
Charles Lewis, United States Army
Robert O'Steen, United States Marines
John Overman, United States Navy
Rufus Patten, United States Army
Buck Pollus, United States Merchant Marines
Jerry Pope, United States Army
Jim Spivey, United States Navy
Paul Taylor, United States Air Force
Harry Walker, United States Marines
Doug Whidden, United States Army

Julius Williams, United States Army
Colquitt County
Patrick McCain, United States Army
Coweta County
Charles Gardner, United States Army
David Prater, United States Army
DeKalb County
Tom Fisher, United States Marines
Eugene McCord, United States Army
Dougherty County
Marvin Mixon, United States Army
Douglas County
Lofton Fouts, United States Army
Echols County
Phil Livermore, United States Navy
Evans County
Henry Bailey, United States Navy
Fannin County
Charles Jinks, III, United States Navy
Fayette County
Frank Dixon, United States Army
Greg Dunn, United States Army
Julia Gainey, United States Air Force
William Gainey, United States Air Force
Floyd County
Bill Gilliland, United States Army
Hugh Atkins, United States Army
Fulton County
Michael Bennett, United States Navy
John Bradberry, United States Marines
Tom Fisher, United States Marines
Derek V. Good, United States Army

John Gordon, United States Air Force
Jack Peevy, United States Army
Joseph Wilkinson, United States Army
Jack Winter, United States Navy
Rick Wolters, United States Navy
Glynn County
R.B. Gentry, United States Marines
Nick Hart, United States Army
Gordon County
Cloe Nave, Georgia Air National Guard
Grady County
Willard Collins, United States Army
Greene County
Mike McLandon, United States Army
Gwinnett County
Bryan Cash, United States Marines
Adrian Costanaez, United States Marines
Wilson Dreger, United States Army
Dewey Earnest, United States Army
Jim Freeman, United States Army
Craig Helf, United States Army
Dennis Loughnane, United States Army
Pete Mitchell, United States Army
Michael Murphy, United States Navy
Marvin Myers, United States Navy
Jose Perez, United States Army
Ken Spencer, United States Navy
Hall County
Dave Nottingham, United States Army
Christopher Meyer, United States Army
Haralson County
H Lamar Hicks, United States Army

Harris County
William McDonald, United States Army
Henry County
William D. Jordan, United States Navy
Houston County
John Boylan, United States Air Force
Jimmy Connell, United States Air Force
Mary Davis, United States Air Force
Barry Segraves, United States Air Force
Lonnie Thomas, United States Air Force
Irwin County
Arnold Parson, United States Army
Jasper County
Sam Goolsby, United States Navy
Jeff Davis County
Arliss Burch, United States Army
Leon Burch, United States Navy
B.H. Claxton, United States Army
Dewayne Page, United States Marines
Larry Page, United States Army
Jones County
James Childs, United States Army
Lamar County
Robert Colston, United States Coast Guard
Elizabeth Colston, United States Coast Guard
Laurens County
Keith Beck, United States Army
Howard Woodard, United States Marines
Lee County
Bruce Austin, United States Army
Liberty County
Edward Colby, United States Army

Long County
Woodrow Mixon, United States Army
Lowndes County
John Patterson, United States Army
Lumpkin County
Randy Griffin, United States Navy
Macon County
William Willingham, United States Army
McIntosh County
Bill Fanning, United States Air Force
Montgomery County
Samuel Surrency, United States Army
Morgan County
Oscar Hanson, United States Marines
Muscogee County
Stephen Boyd, United States Army
Jim Dowden, United States Army
Newton County
Drayton Ballard, United States Army
Hugh Townley, United States Army
Oconee County
Tony Cushenberry, United States Air Force
Paulding County
Ben Grinstead, United States Army
Pickens County
James Hefner, United States Army
Pierce County
Dan Clark, United States Army
Richard McGee, United States Navy
Polk County
Harwell Minschew, United States Army
Michael Sinyard, United States Navy

Rabun County
Frank Bean, United States Air Force
Robert Fink, United States Army
Richmond County
Jim Hussey, United States Marines
Rockdale County
James Taylor, United States Army
Screven County
Paul Stevens, United States Army
Seminole County
Joel T. Smith, United States Air Force
Spalding County
Phil Mouchet, United States Army
Stephens County
John Taylor, United States Air Force
Stewart County
Joe Carter, United States Army
Talbot County
Terry Rumph, United States Army
Taliaferro County
John Allen, United States Army
Glynn Fennell, United States Army
Sam D. Greene, United States Army
Aubrey Harris, United States Army
Robert Kendrick, United States Air Force
Bobby Jones, United States Air Force
George Ledford, United States Army
Dillard Noggle, United States Navy
Harry Reynolds, United States Army

Tattnall County
Johnnie Nails, United States Army
Horse Turner, United States Navy
Lawson Turner, United States Navy
Telfair County
Ernest Dyal, United States Army
Thomas County
John Green, United States Army
Tift County
Jim Golden, United States Army
Joel North, United States Army
Toombs County
James Brewer, United States Marines
Treutlen County
Frank Hudinson, United States Navy
Turner County
Barry Barbee, United States Army
Doug Barbee, United States Army
George Barbee, United States Army
Mark Barbee, United States Army
Upson County
Andrew Penn, United States Army
Walker County
Robert Clark, United States Army
Charles Bledsoe, United States Navy
Walton County
Bobby Boss, United States Army

Ware County
Larry Billinti, United States Army
W.H. Cannington, United States Army
Will Chastain, United States Navy
Steve Elliston, United States Navy
Ellis Hargrove, United States Army
Charles Jenkins, United States Army
Gerald Lang, United States Army
Ronald Lynn, United States Air Force
Steve Parker, United States Air Force
Ellie Royal, United States Navy
Ben Smith, United States Army
Warren County
Laverne McCullough, United States Army
Jim McMichael, United States Army
George Wiley, United States

October 20, 2002

Sonny Returns to Albany
Friday, October 25 - 5:00 pm
Veteran's Park Amphitheater

Sonny is making his final victory statewide tour and will be back in Albany at 5:00 pm on Friday, October 25th at the Veteran's Park Amphitheater next to James Gray Civic Center. Sonny has been to Albany numerous times during his campaign. Southwest Georgia has the ear of Sonny Perdue. Come meet Sonny and bring a friend to meet our next Governor.

The Phones are Ringing for Sonny

Teams of phone callers are meeting each night next week at Albany Travel Agency 2305 Dawson Road from 6:00 to 8:30 to call on behalf of Sonny. We are receiving very positive, friendly, responses. People like Sonny and they are glad to hear from someone who supports him. Come join the party.

October 22, 2002

Friday, October 25 - 5:00 pm
Veteran's Park Amphitheater
Sonny Returns to Albany

Sonny is making his final victory statewide tour and will be back in Albany at 5:00 pm on Friday, October 25th at the Veteran's Park Amphitheater next to James Gray Civic Center. Sonny has been to Albany numerous times during his campaign. Southwest Georgia has the ear of Sonny Perdue. Come meet Sonny and bring a friend to meet our next Governor.

October 26, 2002

Fantastic Crowd Meets Sonny and other Republican Candidates in Sonny's Final Campaign Visit to Albany

Veteran's Park Amphitheater was filled with signs for Sonny Perdue, Saxby Chambliss, Ed Rynders, Steve Stancil, Doug Everett, and other Republican candidates yesterday. WALB TV provided live coverage of the event. Sonny has been to Albany numerous times during the campaign and every event has been a huge success. A Southwest Georgia televised audience saw the enthusiastic cheers and sign waving for Sonny. Sonny's message to the crowd was simple for these last 10 days of the campaign. Keep on doing what you've been doing for the past year and make this final push across the goal line.

Final Days Campaign Opportunities

As we enter in to the final days of the campaign there are opportunities to help. Here are a few:

Phone Banks - they have been going great. We still have available lines at Albany Travel Agency from 6:00 pm - 8:30 pm each night starting back up next Monday. The responses have been great. We have made several thousand calls and still have about two thousand to go. Come join us.

Sign Wavers - Thursday, Friday, and Monday we want people waving signs for Sonny at key high traffic areas. We will want teams of at least 2 at each location.

Poll Watchers - The Republican Party is asking for volunteers as poll watchers. Gary Smith, Dougherty County Republican Chairman will need to register poll watchers with election officials no later than 3 days prior to the election. We will be sending a separate e-mail regarding this important subject.

Sign Wavers at Precincts - Key precincts need people waving at people who go into vote. Studies have shown that some people decide at the last minute and your smiling face and friendly wave, may very well win a vote for Sonny.

Besides the organized activities, just keep on talking up Sonny to your friends and family. If you have friends you haven't talked with in a while across Georgia, use this as a good opportunity to give them a call and see how they have been doing.

Sonny's advisors tell us that things are looking really good. The TV ads are having the expected positive impact. The advertisement with President Bush begins soon. The general population is starting to think about the election and they like what they see in Sonny.

October 29, 2002

In the final days of this historic campaign, Sonny is moving all over the state in the old-fashioned way of touching voters, listening, and asking for their votes. While Sonny is strong on the "high-touch" side of the campaign, he is also hitting the television markets on the "high-tech" side of modern day campaigning. The latest ad with the endorsement of President Bush is a home run. Check it out at Sonny's main web site: www.votesonny.com.

Use Push Cards with Halloween Treats

Here's a great idea to promote Sonny. Put a push card for Sonny in the bag with a Halloween treat. Parents will check out all the candy and treats and learn something about Sonny. Call Gregg Jones at 435-2285 to get a supply.

Innovative Ideas From the Next Generation

This has got to be one of the most innovative ideas of the entire campaign and it came from a 9 year-old. You saw it right. It isn't a typo. A 9 year old. With Halloween just around the corner, this 9 year old said, "I want to dress up like a Sonny Perdue Billboard." We have got to get a picture of that one.

Letter to the Albany Herald People's Forum

Dear Editor,

Look into his eyes and you see a sincere, honest, man who simply desires to serve. Over the past year, thousands of people across Georgia have looked into the eyes of Sonny Perdue as they shared their ideas, hopes, and dreams. They saw a man who didn't fit the mold of a typical politician. They saw a man who really cares about them and their ideas. Sonny and his wife, Mary, have had a direct influence in the lives of young people through foster parenting. Their son has committed his life to the ministry and is a student in seminary. Sonny's heritage is one of service.

Two words sum up Sonny Perdue – trust and respect. He is a man who rose to the highest position in the Georgia Senate, not by political power plays, but by showing respect to his fellow Senators and gaining their trust. Sonny recognizes that not everyone will agree on an issue, but he has a gift of leading people to come up with a positive solution that benefits everyone.

Sonny leads by serving, listening, and setting an example of working together to accomplish positive goals. One of those positive goals was the constitutional amendment Sonny co-sponsored in 1998 to protect and secure the HOPE Scholarship. One wouldn't know that by watching some commercials.

Sonny's candidacy is about people, not about power. Sonny trusts and respects the people of Georgia. Trust Sonny Perdue with your vote for him as our next Governor on November 5.[39]

Donald E. Cole
Albany, Georgia

November 1, 2002

This has got to win the prize for most innovative promotion of Sonny.
Robert came up with the idea of trick-or-treat as a Sonny Perdue Billboard!

Telephone Campaign Wrapping Up

The volunteers making phone calls for Dougherty and Lee County are wrapping up the calls. The team placed approximately 6000 phone calls to homes of voters in Dougherty and Lee County. We sent out hundreds of packets of information with personal notes to those who were undecided and wanted more information. The calls have been extremely positive. Hundreds of Democrats said they were voting for Sonny! Amazingly, we didn't find a single Republican indicating a leaning toward Roy Barnes.

Although the official canvassing is completed, you keep calling your friends. Make a list of friends and family across the state and call them this weekend to get them out to vote on Tuesday!

Sign Waving Kicks Off

As the telephone campaign is wrapping up, the sign waving campaign kicked off yesterday. Teams stood at Bank of Lee County on US 19 at Ledo Road, Dawson Road near 3rd and Magnolia, Westover near Old Dawson, at the corner of Jefferson and Philema, and at the corner of Gordon and Slappey waving signs for Sonny Perdue and Saxby Chambliss. Today the team will add to the locations, the American Outdoors on US 82 just West of the by-pass. All major areas of Albany and Lee County were covered from 4:30 - 6:00 pm during the heaviest traffic times. The teams will be waving signs again today and Monday. We are also staffing up for sign waving at voting precincts on Tuesday. If you want to help, just reply to this e-mail.

History in the Making

On Tuesday, November 5, we will make history when Georgians elect the first Republican Governor since Reconstruction. You have all been a key part. When you forward an e-mail update, make a phone call, put a yard sign in your yard, place a bumper-sticker on the car, or tell a friend that you are voting for Sonny - you are part of a vast army writing a new chapter in the history books. In Dougherty/Lee counties alone we have had at least 400 people involved in this campaign in some way - yard signs, bumper stickers, phone calls, waving signs, giving out information, and so forth. On behalf of Sonny, the Dougherty/Lee County team thanks you for your willingness to stand publicly for Sonny. Keep up the good work.

November 3, 2002

Sprinting to the Finish Line

Last Thursday and Friday in key areas of Dougherty and Lee County thousands were greeted with a friendly smile, an enthusiastic wave, and Sonny and Saxby Signs. The response was overwhelmingly positive in every area - South Albany, Northwest Albany, Lee County. Pickup trucks to Cadillacs were honking and showing support for Sonny. We'll be out again on Monday and then on Tuesday at key precincts.

Dougherty/Lee Welcomes President Bush to Savannah

When President Bush arrived in Savannah last Saturday, Don Cole of Albany represented Southwest Georgia as one of eight official greeters. Among the eight greeters were Nancy Coverdell, Former Senator and Ambassador Mac Mattingly and his wife, Leslie, Calder Clay, Candidate for 3rd District US House of Representatives, Max Burns, Candidate for 12th District US House of Representatives. Don passed on greetings from Southwest Georgia and told President Bush that we appreciate all that he is doing.

All the Work Comes Down to 12 Hours on Tuesday

People across Georgia have worked very hard these past months. When we started earlier this year, it was "Sonny Who?"

72 hours from now it will be Governor-Elect Perdue. You have caught Sonny's vision and have spread the word in a grass roots campaign that will go down in the history books and political science textbooks. Sonny has won the hearts of people across our great state. You have invested a part of your life into a cause that supercedes politics as usual. This campaign has been summed up in a simple phrase - "Power of the People versus the People of Power." Over 400 people across Dougherty and Lee County have formally invested a part of their lives in this campaign. Some supported with finances. Some supported by using their property for key sign locations. Some supported by making telephone calls. Some supported by going door to door. Some supported by waving signs. Countless others have invested themselves informally by talking to their friends and neighbors. In every case, people supported Sonny because they wanted to support Sonny, not because they felt coerced to support Sonny. In the first days of the campaign, Sonny made this comment, "The difference in those who contribute to me and those who contribute to Roy is that I know I can count on the votes of those who contribute to me." That still holds true today.

The work isn't over though. In fact, the key to all the work will be in the 12 hours between 7:00 am and 7:00 pm next Tuesday. All the talk, all the work, all the effort are summed up when you enter the voting booth and cast your vote for Sonny Perdue. That is the only poll that matters. Call your friends to go vote. Offer a ride to the polls. The key to this election as with every election, lies in getting out the vote of those who support your cause. Let's go make history. See you at the polls.

November 11, 2002

Southwest Georgians Celebrate at the Hyatt
L-R - Leslie Cole, Donald Cole, Jackson Murphy, Sheryl Gamble,
T. Gamble, Dotty Jones, Jack Jones, Gregg Jones

Reflections on an Historic Campaign

I am sitting in a cabin in the mountains as I write this final Dougherty/Lee County update to the Sonny Perdue for Governor campaign. Several months ago Leslie and I planned to go to Atlanta to be with Sonny and his supporters from across the state on election night, then go straight to the mountains to decompress from the past year. The only drawback was that the final update would have to wait a few days.

People started flowing into the Grand Ballroom of the Hyatt around 7:00 pm. Donald and Leslie Cole, T. & Sheryl Gamble, Gregg and Jami Jones with their young son, Cameron, Jack and Dotty Jones, Jackson Murphy and Corinna Magelund on Sonny's staff, represented Dougherty and Lee counties and the 2nd Congressional District campaign committees. There was an air of excitement in the room as Sonny came out and spoke the first time.

The room was set up with a large projector and laptop computer linked to the Georgia Secretary of State web site. The first returns began to come in from Fulton County. Roy Barnes held a lead at 51% as the returns came in. Around 45 minutes to an hour into the posting of returns, there was a loud cheer when the screen flashed up the new numbers and Sonny took the lead with over 50%. Sonny never dropped below 50% for the rest of the night. When the screen showed 88% of the returns in and Sonny holding a strong lead, the crowd started the familiar chant that has followed Sonny across this state, "Sonny, Sonny, Sonny, Sonny." A few minutes later Sonny came out and announced that about 10 minutes ago he had received a call from President Bush and then about 2 minutes ago he received a very gracious call from Governor Barnes congratulating him on victory. The place went bonkers. We had accomplished the impossible.

On Wednesday morning, I began to call those who worked so hard in this campaign to thank them. One call in particular was to Lila Faye Everson at Palmyra Nursing Home. Mrs. Everson's great nephew is Rev. Mike Everson who served several years as co-pastor of 2nd Baptist Church in Warner Robins where Sonny is a member. On one of his trips to Albany, Sonny made a stop by Palmyra Nursing Home to see Mrs. Everson. There were no reporters, no cameras, and no big fanfare – just Sonny, Mrs. Everson, and myself. After a short visit, Sonny prayed for Mrs. Everson and went back to his campaign. His visit to Mrs. Everson wasn't campaign – it was Sonny's typical quiet, humble, ministry. Every time I talk with Mrs. Everson she asks about Sonny and wants me to let him know that she is praying for him every day. Mrs. Everson put a Sonny Country poster on her wall to let everyone at Palmyra know where she stood. She made sure that she got her absentee ballot in the mail. As I spoke with Mrs.

Everson on Wednesday morning, for the first time I felt a lump in my throat and tears welled in my eyes. She and people just like her won this election. She had no money to offer, no powerful position of influence, no favors to call in. She had neither carrot nor stick. In Dougherty and Lee Counties, hundreds did just what Mrs. Everson did – they offered what they could and stood with Sonny. Some supported financially. Some put a sign on their property or a bumper sticker on their vehicle. Some made phone calls. Some wrote letters. Some waved signs. Some made sure that a friend or family member got to the polls or got in that absentee ballot. This was truly a victory for the people. Sonny put it best in his victory speech when he said, "David still wins."

Now, the campaign is over and it is time to accept the responsibility, which "We the People" have demanded. A monolithic, centralized committee did not run this campaign and a monolithic, centralized government will not govern this state. You will be a key part in pulling people together to meet the challenges and tremendous opportunities we face as Georgians. Let me give you one example. Education and SAT scores were a major issue in the campaign. You can find a high school student and offer to be an encourager and motivator in helping that student prepare for the exam. If you don't know a student, then call a friend, a minister, a civic club, a teacher, a principal and let them know that you want to encourage a student – just one student - to be the best they can be in school and to be well prepared for the SAT. It doesn't take a bureaucracy in Atlanta for you to take that one simple step which will revolutionize our educational system. Sonny will set the vision. The state can't hire enough people to solve every problem and meet every challenge and Sonny cannot do it alone.

When Georgians elected Sonny Perdue they showed the nation that grassroots campaigning was more than just an old phrase - it still works. Now we have the opportunity to show the nation that government "By the People" is not just an old phrase – it still works. May God richly bless you. Let's get to work.

Donald E. Cole
Dougherty County Co-Chair
Sonny Perdue for a New Georgia

Epilogue - Life's Bottom Line

Thank you for allowing me to share the excitement of Sonny's historical grassroots victory as the first Republican elected to be Georgia's Governor in over 130 years. Winning is exhilarating. Whether it be hooking the big one while fishing alone, making the hole-in-one with a foursome, winning a championship game played before thousands, or winning an election with over a million votes – winning is exhilarating. Winning fulfills a need of experiencing feelings of importance, success, achievement, value, and worth. All of these are important human needs. There is one human need; however, that winning will never meet. In fact, no public official, no celebrity, no achievement, and no other human being can meet your need of having a right relationship with God.

You have spent time with me walking through an exciting story of Sonny's big win. Will you give me another five minutes to share a few paragraphs that could change your destiny for eternity? I call this, "Life's Bottom Line."

Take a walk outside and look around. Try to count the different forms of life – plants, animals, insects, and so on. Now start breaking those down into various groups – pine trees, oak trees, grass, flowers, dogs, cats, horses, birds. You get the idea. We live in a marvelous, magnificent, creation. The wonder of our world and our universe is too great for words. Let me get to my point. This creation did not "just happen" by itself. The Master Designer put this all together and maintains the delicate balance that keeps it running. The same One who created our amazing universe created human beings with the ability to have a relationship – a personal relationship - with Him.

The first humans, Adam and Eve, were perfect in every way. They were not humped over, knuckle-dragging, cave people, they were perfect specimens of humanity.[40] They lived in a perfect world in a perfect relationship with God. They had only one rule – do not eat fruit from a single, specific tree.[41] Why would God have such a rule? The answer to that is simple. In order to have a personal relationship, either person must have the ability to choose for or against the relationship. God gave Adam and Eve the ability to choose to obey or disobey Him. Adam and Eve's choice broke the perfect relationship with God and opened the door for sin and death to enter the world. The perfect spiritual life in them died leaving an empty void ruled by fear. That void has passed on from generation to generation.

The empty void in each life is a condition called sin. Sin is not just a behavior pattern; it is a condition that is shared by every human being. The Bible puts it plainly, "for all have sinned and fall short of the glory of God." (Romans 3:23) Our tendency is to put sin in the category of behavior alone. Just as the disease of cancer is not a behavior, neither is sin just a behavior – it is a condition with a fatal prognosis.

When God created Adam and Eve, He desired to have a personal relationship with them. They rejected God, but He did not reject them. God's plan was simple. He would pay the price for sin and offer a renewed relationship. He put His plan into action and over 2000 years ago, in the little Middle Eastern village of Bethlehem, a miracle took place when God's son, Jesus Christ, was born to a virgin named Mary. That baby grew up and lived a perfect life, in a perfect relationship with God. He taught God's truth, healed the sick, made the blind to see, the lame to walk, the deaf to hear, and the dead to live. He offered Himself as the perfect and only payment for sin when He was crucified and died on a cross. Three days later, another miracle took place. God raised Jesus Christ from the grave. He accomplished the plan, paying the price for sin, and offering a renewed relationship with God. The Bible says, "But God demonstrates His own love toward us, in that while we were yet sinners, Christ died for us." (Romans 5:8)

You came into this world with a void in your life that can only be filled in a personal relationship with God. No achievement, no matter how great, will fill that void. The void is a condition and it is eternally fatal. But there is good news. There is a cure. Remember what I wrote three paragraphs ago? "In order to have a personal relationship, either person must have the ability to choose for or against the relationship." The good news is that God has made his choice – and His choice is for, not against, a relationship with you. He makes this offer as a free gift to everyone. The Bible puts it like this, "the free gift of God is eternal life in Christ Jesus our Lord." (Romans 6:23) and "Whoever will call upon the name of the Lord will be saved." (Romans 10:13)

Let's make this personal. Do you have a personal relationship with God right now? God desires to have that relationship with you. It is no accident that you are still reading this. He is reaching out to you and calling you by name. Let Him fill that void that no one else can fill. Jesus said, "I am the way, the truth, and the life; no one comes to the Father, but through Me." (John 14:6) There are no magic words, no magic formulas. Here is the idea in a simple prayer: "Jesus, I am a sinner. I cannot save myself. I want a relationship with you and I accept your gift of eternal life." God knows your heart. He will take it from there.

Life's bottom line is that some day, you will take your last breath and your heart will beat its last beat. You will step into eternity. At that moment, your political party, for whom you voted, how much you own, or what position you hold, will matter nothing to you. The only thing that will matter for eternity is your personal relationship with Jesus Christ. That, my friend, is life's bottom line.

Endnotes

[1] Sean Hannity used this term in his syndicated radio talk show on November 6, 2002.

[2] E-Mail County Chair Update from Sonny Perdue Campaign – October 2, 2002.

[3] State of Georgia web site:
www.legis.state.ga.us/legis/1997_98/house/gass18.htm.

[4] State of Georgia web site:
www.legis.state.ga.us/legis/1997_00/house/gass18.htm.

[5] I read of a similar object lesson in a book that I received as a high school graduation present May 30, 1971 from the Woman's Society of Christian Service on behalf of the Bonaire United Methodist Church. The University of Hard Knocks by Ralph Parlette, published by Brownlow Publishing, Fort Worth, Texas. Copyright renewed 1966.

[6] WFXL nightly news broadcast November 4, 2002.

[7] Sean Hannity used this term in his syndicated radio talk show on November 6, 2002.

[8] Albany Herald People's Forum – February 5, 2002.

[9] E-Mail press release from Sonny Perdue Campaign – April 18, 2002.

[10] E-Mail press release from Sonny Perdue Campaign – April 19, 2002.

[11] E-Mail press release from Sonny Perdue Campaign – April 29, 2002.

[12] Editorial in Macon Telegraph and News – May 24, 2002.

[13] Editorial by Jim Wooten in the Atlanta Journal-Constitution – May 24, 2002.

[14] Atlanta Journal-Constitution – May 23, 2002.

[15] Neal Boortz – www.boortz.com - Nealz Nuze– May 23, 2002.

[16] CapitolImpact.com – Georgia Report May 22, 2002.

[17] E-Mail County Chair Update from Sonny Perdue Campaign – May 30, 2002.

[18] E-Mail County Chair Update from Sonny Perdue Campaign – June 11, 2002.

[19] E-Mail County Chair Update from Sonny Perdue Campaign – June 15, 2002.

[20] E-Mail County Chair Update from Sonny Perdue Campaign – July 15, 2002.

[21] E-Mail press release from Sonny Perdue Campaign – April 19, 2002.

[22] E-Mail County Chair Update from Sonny Perdue Campaign – July 31, 2002.

[23] Albany Herald Squawkbox – August 4, 2002.

[24] Quotes from Atlanta Journal and Marietta Daily Journal contained in e-Mail County Chair Update from Sonny Perdue Campaign – August 7, 2002.

[25] Atlanta Journal-Constitution editorial – August 7, 2002

[26] Marietta Daily Journal editorial – August 7, 2002.

[27] E-Mail County Chair Update from Sonny Perdue Campaign – August 8, 2002.

[28] E-Mail County Chair Update from Sonny Perdue Campaign – August 9, 2002.

[29] Savannah Morning News – August 9, 2002.

[30] Albany Herald, People's Forum – August 8, 2002.

[31] E-Mail County Chair Update from Sonny Perdue Campaign – August 17, 2002.

[32] Albany Herald, People's Forum – August 19, 2002.

[33] WALB TV August 23, 2002. Web site link:
http://www.walb.com/global/Story.asp?s=906884.

[34] E-Mail received from Joe Cornelius, Perdue for a New Georgia Warner Robins Campaign Office – October 4, 2002.

[35] E-Mail County Chair Update from Sonny Perdue Campaign – October 2, 2002.

[36] E-Mail County Chair Update from Sonny Perdue Campaign – October 3, 2002.

[37] E-Mail County Chair Update from Sonny Perdue Campaign – October 9, 2002.

[38] E-Mail County Chair Update from Sonny Perdue Campaign – October 15, 2002.

[39] This letter was published in the Albany Herald People's Forum – November 2, 2002.

[40] This description is found in the book Peace With God by Reverend Billy Graham. I recommend this book to everyone.

[41] Genesis 2:16-17